BOUNCING BACK

How to Handle Setbacks in Your Work and Personal Life

ANDREW J. DuBRIN

PaperJacks LTD.

Toronto   **New York**

PaperJacks

One of a series of books
published by PaperJacks Ltd.

BOUNCING BACK

How to Handle Setbacks in Your Work and Personal Life

To Drew

Published by arrangement with Prentice-Hall, Inc., Englewood Cliffs,
New Jersey 07632
Prentice-Hall edition published 1982

PaperJacks edition published September 1984

Second Printing August 1985

Cover design: Brant Cowie/Artplus Ltd.

ISBN 0-7701-0318-9
Copyright © 1982 by Prentice-Hall, Inc.
All rights reserved
Printed in Canada

CONTENTS

PREFACE

Several years ago, in the midst of a cocktail party, an old friend and colleague asked me what topic I was investigating these days. I replied, "How people cope with hard times in their life." My friend countered, "Aren't we all wondering about the same thing?" He had a good point. Although usually unstated, most people are trying to figure out how to handle hard times, whether they be temporary or permanent. Despite the ubiquity of the problem, very little has been published about the general topic of dealing with different types of adversity.

Most of the published information about bouncing back from downturns in life deals with specific topics, such as how to cope with divorce, death, or bankruptcy. One troublesome aspect of books and articles of this nature is that they are discouraging, dealing more with problems than with solutions.

My belief is that the world needs an upbeat guide that provides suggestions for handling a wide variety of losses, adversities, and reversals. *Bouncing Back* is written to fill that need. The strategies, techniques, and mental attitudes presented in this book are designed to help people overcome the potential adverse consequences of setback and avoid the feeling of having been defeated. This book is not designed to empty mental hospitals or to replace psychotherapy and counseling. Anyone facing setback, who has reasonable control over his or her emotions and actions, should derive some benefit from these strategies.

This book is organized around specific kinds of setback. These include annoyances, financial trouble, illness and injury, loss of personal relationships, and defeat in competition. Nevertheless, many of the suggestions for dealing with one type of adversity will also work for other types.

The basic source of information for this book is my judgment and experience as a professor and psychologist, buttressed by several hundred case histories gathered specifically as research material for this book. In addition, some published sources are quoted.

Brief, italicized comments are presented throughout that tie the strategies and tactics to psychological and behavioral concepts. I hope these brief analyses will make this book suitable for use in courses such as the psychology of personal adjustment and human relations. Simultaneously, by setting these comments apart, I hope they will not interfere with the flow of the book for those readers not concerned about the tie-in of bouncing-back strategies to established theoretical concepts.

My primary thanks go to three of my past research assistants, Mike Kretovic, Tom Schoder, and Dick Oswald. All three men collected case histories and gathered whatever scant information has been published on the topic. I thank the hundreds of my students at the College of Business of the Rochester Institute of Technology who have given their physical and mental energy to this project. Thanks also to K. Lois Smith, my manuscript typist, and Lynn Krenzer, who enthusiastically carried out some necessary clerical tasks.

Finally, I thank all those who created circumstances whereby bouncing back was a personal necessity for me. Without these people and the circumstances they created, my writing on this topic might have been too sterile and detached. The writing of this book has converted all my past antagonists and detractors into collaborators.

Andrew J. DuBrin, Ph.D., is a psychologist and professor of behavioral sciences at the Rochester Institute of Technology College of Business, where he also serves as a staff chairman. In addition to numerous appearances on radio and TV talk shows, he has lectured extensively and written several books and articles including *Effective Business Psychology* and *Human Relations for Career and Personal Success* (Prentice-Hall, Inc.).

chapter one
BOUNCING BACK

When things go wrong, as they sometimes will,
And the road you're trudging on seems all uphill,
When the funds are low and the debts are high,
And you want to smile, but have to sigh,
When cares are pressing you down a bit,
Rest, if you must, but never quit!

Life is strange with its twists and turns,
As every one of us sometimes learns,
And many a failure turns about
When you may have won, had you stuck it out;
Don't give up, though the pace seems slow—
You may succeed with one more blow.

Success is failure turned inside out—
The silver tints in the clouds of doubt—
And you never can tell how close you are,
It may be near when it seems afar;
So stick to the fight when you're hardest hit—
It's when things seem worst that you must not quit.

Author unknown

Why are some people so successful in overcoming setbacks while others become fearful or despondent? How do some people shrug off catastrophic events when others facing similar circumstances become

1

immobilized? Why do some people flick away everyday annoyances, yet others are emotionally drained by them and therefore unable to deal with bigger issues? I've been sufficiently intrigued by these questions to devote several years of research time to finding some answers. Apparently those who bounce back in life live by the wisdom of the poem just presented. Of equal importance, they seem to use straightforward, practical strategies to help circumvent defeat.

This book contains over one hundred strategies and techniques for bouncing back from setback, disappointment, and hard times. For convenience, I have organized these techniques according to the type of problem encountered, such as financial woes, being dumped by a spouse or lover, or getting axed on the job. Let's begin with the bounce-back tactics of six people, each of whom successfully overcame a different type of problem.

A LOVING HUSBAND GETS DUMPED

With tears in his eyes and a lump in his throat, Tony lamented,

> It came as such a shock. I thought we were the most solid couple in our apartment building. I loved Bridgit. She was everything I always wanted in a woman: bright, attractive, and understanding. She had all kinds of talents and interests—painting, cooking, racquetball—you name it.
>
> I've known Bridgit ten years. We dated for one year, lived together for three, and were married for six years. After three years of marriage we had Jeanne. The fabulous little kid is as good looking as her mom. The three of us did all sorts of things together. While the other guys were out on Sunday afternoon playing softball, I was on a picnic or a balcony cookout with my wife and daughter. I thought I was appreciated.
>
> About six months ago, I began to notice some bad vibrations in our relationship, which seemed to be coming from Bridgit. I loved her as much as always, but she began to withdraw a little from sex. Nothing drastic, but a little less desire. She also began to spend more time visiting with her mother and friends.
>
> I asked her a few times if anything was wrong. Bridgit said that nothing was really wrong; she was feeling a little moody these days. She said that she would be back to normal in no time.

Back to normal never came. One night while we were watching the 10 o'clock news, Bridget turned to me and asked me to shut off the TV. There was something urgent she had to tell me. I thought that Bridget or Jeanne were sick or Bridgit was pregnant or had gotten a speeding ticket. How wrong I was.

Bridgit told me that it was all over between us. She said she couldn't handle the monotony of being married to me any longer. She told me that she had no hard feelings, but that she and I were no longer suited to each other.

I was so shocked, I was speechless. Unfortunately, Bridgit's talk about us being unsuited was just the preliminary shock. She then told me that she had fallen in love with an older, well-established man. She and Jeanne would be moving to his country estate about twenty-five miles from our home. She was quitting her job and going to pursue painting fulltime.

After ten minutes of conversation, I realized my whole world had changed. Instead of Tony, his beautiful wife, and child, it would be Tony alone in the apartment eating TV dinners. What would I tell my parents, my friends, the people at work?

After several weeks the shockwaves wore off and Tony gained a better perspective on his problem. His life was not over; he was still Jeanne's father. Bridgit had not left his life entirely. With full cooperation from his wife, he established a healthy visitation schedule with Jeanne. Since money was not an issue with Bridgit, Tony was able to pay enough child support to maintain his self-respect as a parent, yet not be disabled financially.

Nor was Tony's life with Bridgit ended. After the sting of bitterness and resentment had subsided, Tony came to realize that he and Bridgit would be having plenty of contact over the years. They still would have to hold discussions about all major matters relating to their daughter, but Bridgit and Tony could still maintain a friendship with each other.

Tony soon realized that his relationships with women were beginning, not ending. As a thirty-two year old unattached male, there would be ample opportunities for social life ahead. The first woman he approached for a date made a comment that helped Tony bounce back to reality. Fumbling Tony said to her, "Before this conversation goes further, I must tell you something important about myself. I'm separated and I have a child." The compassionate woman said, "Don't worry about it. Every other person in this place is either separated or divorced. Join the crowd."

AN EVICTED RESTAURANT OWNER
TRANSFERS HER SKILLS

Gwen had invested a good portion of her life savings in a restaurant.[1] Starting from scratch in a small college town, the Gourmet Shoppe developed into a prosperous, low-budget meal place for college students and townspeople. During the first three years of ownership, Gwen devoted an average of sixty-five hours a week into making the Gourmet Shoppe a success. A solid clientele had been established, and Gwen looked forward to reducing her personal workload.

As lease-renewal time approached a telephone inquiry to the landlord brought forth some devastating news. "I'm sorry," said the landlord, "I won't be renewing your lease. I've sold the building and the new owners don't want any tenants. Maybe they're going to build a shopping mall. Whatever their plans, you have sixty days to get off the premises. Thanks for being such a good tenant over the three years."

Stunned, but not immobilized, Gwen surveyed the situation. She estimated that she had a $10,000 food inventory and a $13,000 equipment debt. The sudden shock of being out of business after working hard for three years, combined with the prospects of unemployment, seemed overwhelming. Gwen carefully evaluated the options facing her. Two hours of tough thinking yielded a workable plan.

Part one of Gwen's plan was to keep the restaurant open long enough to deplete most of the food inventory. She juggled the menu to push items she had in surplus, including cod fish croquettes as a $3.75 special. She ordered just enough of the basics such as eggs, milk, and bread to keep the Gourmet Shoppe a plausible place to eat. While depleting the food inventory, Gwen sold enough restaurant equipment to pay off the bank note.

In addition to phasing out the restaurant, Gwen investigated other employment opportunities. She applied for and received, a position as the manager of a department-store restaurant. She liked the restaurant business, and here was a chance to run one without risk. The store offered a solid benefit package including medical insurance, vacations (a rarity for a restaurant owner), a retirement plan, and profit sharing.

Asked if she would want to to open a Gourmet Shoppe again, Gwen replied, "I doubt it. I've been that route once. While it was fun, I would not want those headaches again. I parlayed my experience into a cushy spot and made a sound decision."

4

Gwen did make a sound decision in her particular circumstance. You might ask why she didn't try to find a new location for the Gourmet Shoppe. Intuitively she knew that other locations available to her at a sensible price were poor risks. They were not in convenient walking distance to the campus. Gwen also recognized that although her restaurant was to be demolished, her basic management skills remained with her. She rationally found a way of transferring her skills to a new location. She bounced back by shifting her act, not cancelling it.

A BLINDED HUNTER BECOMES AN ATTORNEY

At age nineteen, Wendell was a serious-minded and athletic college student.[2] He was performing well academically and had hopes of becoming a successful attorney. One Thanksgiving vacation, Wendell agreed to go deer hunting with three old friends. They headed into the woods at four o'clock in the morning hoping to find some deer at daybreak. The foursome never did shoot a deer that day. A zealous hunter spotted the four of them and opened fire, thinking he had spotted a deer. A bullet ricocheted off a tree adjacent to Wendell. Shrapnel sprayed into his face, blinding Wendell instantly. His huntmates administered first aid as best they could, then brought him to a hospital emergency room in a nearby town.

Wendell woke up the next morning still in darkness. Optimistic by nature, he assumed that his affliction was temporary. The young college student's optimism was dampened when the attending physician told him he was blinded for life. Wendell was terrified about the consequences of blindness. He felt an overwhelming sadness when he realized he never again would see the beauty of the world.

At first smitten with self-pity, within a month Wendell began to realize that he was still the same ambitious, determined person. Fate had taken away his vision, but not all of his solid inner qualities. "If other blind people live full lives, why can't I?" Wendell asked himself.

That afternoon Wendell took the first real step toward his personal renaissance. He asked for an appointment with the hospital therapist so he might begin to learn how to function as a blind person in a sighted world. Wendell attacked each day with the same vigor he used in his sighted life. "My number one goal in life," he told his parents, "is to take advantage of every learning opportunity open to a blind person." With a remarkably rapid rate of progress, Wendell learned to read braille and get around in the outside world with the help of a cane and a leader German shepherd. To the amusement of himself and his friends, Wendell shortly began to refer to his dog Benson and himself as "we."

With the physical help and emotional support of his friends, family, and rehabilitation therapists, Wendell returned to college. He only missed one semester. Thirty years later Wendell is a successful lawyer and a city court judge. He walks to work every day, assisted by his latest leader dog, a golden retriever also named Benson.

His personal life is as full as his professional life. With the aid of friends, and a visually handicapped wife, Wendell is still athletic. He skis, plays golf, and swims. For serenity, he performs gardening chores such as clipping the shrubs. His neighbors kid Wendell about having the best trimmed evergreens on the block.

What bounce-back strategy was used by Wendell, the blinded youth who ultimately became a city court judge? He used the only strategy that made sense to him at the time. Instead of feeling defeated and cut-off from leading a full life, Wendell allowed his best character traits to shine through while facing adversity. The wayward bullet removed Wendell's sight, not his amibtion, perserverance, or seriousness of purpose.

AN INJURED CARPENTER WISELY INVESTS HIS DOWN TIME

When he was fifty-eight years old, carpenter Alex fell twenty-five feet from a scaffold and broke both his hands and wrists.[3] Considering his age and the extent of his injuries, he was forced into early retirement. While he was convalescing at home, Alex's wife persuaded him to keep his hands occupied with some kind of rehabilitative therapy. Alex hit upon the common sense idea of entering contests that required filling out entry forms and clipping the coupons. The writing and snipping seemed well suited to restoring dexterity to his broken hands and wrists.

Alex proceeded to enter over thirty contests per year. His success was modest until one day he finally hit it big winning a Jaguar worth about $37,000 in today's market. This particular contest, sponsored by

Teacher's Scotch, drew 156,000 entries from New York State alone. One of Alex's blanks—he submitted approximately ten dozen entries—was drawn at random by an independent judging organization.

In the past, Alex noted, he has never won anything but "a few small items, although I've averaged between seventy-five and one hundred entries per contest. I figure the writing exercise did me a world of good, however." Alex is firmly convinced that his self-designed therapy prevented potential amputation of one of his hands.

Presently, Alex has about a seventy-five percent recovery on the use of his hands and wrists. He and his wife are in good spirits and getting by financially due to selling the Jaguar. Alex's story has two good lessons for bouncing back, especially in health-related setbacks. First, if you want to win something, take the necessary steps to multiply your odds of winning. Filling in hundreds of entry blanks obviously increases your odds at being chosen the winner. Second, you need more than immediate medical attention and optimism to recover from an injury. You may have to choose a daily activity that will help you ease your way back into close to normal functioning. For Alex, it was clipping out and filling entry blanks. For another person, it might mean walking five miles a day to overcome a back injury.

A FIREFIGHTER COMBATS PANIC

On a warm July 4th evening, Bob's fire station was called to respond to a fire in an inner city building.[4] When the fire company arrived they immediately signaled for more help because the building was fully engulfed in flames. The firefighters tried to battle the fire from the outside of the building, but realized stronger actions would have to be taken. Experience told Bob and his partner that the fire would have to be battled from inside the building. The two men grabbed a hose, went inside, and headed up the stairs toward the attic.

Heat and smoke swirled around the rooms. Somehow, Bob's partner thought that Bob had turned back; therefore he left with the hose. Bob had not left, however, and believed that his partner was behind him. Bob crawled through a small opening in a closet and stumbled up the stairs to the attic. He was attempting to let the smoke and heat escape to prevent the fire from intensifying.

At the moment the walls burst into flames, Bob's oxygen tanks emitted a buzzing sound. The ominous signal meant that the tanks now contained only a two-minute supply of oxygen. Bob suddenly realized he was alone in the attic. As he called for help, the attic now filled with smoke, became hotter. Because of the thick smoke and the debris on the attic floor, Bob found it impossible to locate the small opening he had used as an entrance.

Once outside, his partner notified the other firefighters that Bob was trapped inside. Their response was immediate. The firefighting team scaled the ladder and axed a hole in the roof. Bob was spotted in the flaming attic but a major obstacle became apparent. The team needed more time to make the hole large enough to extricate Bob, who was burdened by the bulky oxygen tank on his back. At this moment his oxygen supply was almost down to death-inducing zero. Since they could not pull Bob through the hole, they had no choice but to let him fall back into the flames.

Meanwhile, another veteran of the fire department entered the still-flaming building. With remarkable speed he crawled up the stairs and located the small opening to the attic. Employing the reflexes of a true firefighting professional, he located Bob. He realized that Bob's oxygen tank was empty and that he was severely burned. The veteran dragged Bob out of the building and called for emergency medical attention.

When the damage was assessed it was discovered that Bob suffered second- and third-degree burns over twenty percent of his body, primarily on his arms and legs. He was taken to the nationally acclaimed burn unit of a local hospital. Bob underwent months of painful treatment. Bob has been back on active duty for five years. He gives his own account of how he handled the double adversity of a close-to-death encounter and his burn rehabilitation:

> When my oxygen tank signaled that I only had a few minutes remaining, there were a couple of important things I had to do to stay alive. Immediately, I realized that the less oxygen I used, the more supply I would have remaining. So it was a life or death matter that I didn't panic. I breathed as calmly as I possibly could. If I had panicked, I would have used up my last amount of oxygen in only a few seconds. By staying calm I actually was buying time while I awaited help.

Another important decision was to leave on my mask and tank even though it was empty and hindered my being pulled out through the small hole in the roof. The hole was too small to pull me through, so the other firemen had no choice but to let me fall back into the flames. My thoughts at the moment were that by leaving on the tank and mask, I would protect my throat and lungs from serious internal injury. I therefore was able to protect myself until I was finally freed.

The attitude I had at the hospital was simply not to give up hope. I realized it was going to be a long journey back. I figured that a positive attitude would help me fight my way back on the road to recovery.

Courageous firefighter Bob thus relied on two key strategies to deal with potentially fatal adversity. In the face of death he resolved to overcome the panic symptom of breathing hard or shouting for help. His feat was all the more remarkable because until only recently, scientists have believed that you cannot voluntarily control your emotions under heavy stress conditions. While recuperating from burns, Bob called into play a strategy used by most people who overcome a serious accident or illness—he refused to give up hope.

A MEMBER OF CONGRESS ENTERS BY ANOTHER DOOR

Young Sam Templeton wanted to follow his father's footsteps and someday be elected to the United States Congress.[5] While still in high school, he formulated the logical plan of majoring in political science at college. He then would attend law school, pass the state bar exam, and begin a career as a lawyer. He shared the popular misconception that being an attorney is an almost indispensable requirement for being elected to congress.

Although a better-than-average student, Sam was not accepted into an accredited law school. He was on many waiting lists but could never quite get that final letter of acceptance. Sam brought his tale of woe to a trusted old professor. She suggested that Sam might consider obtaining a Master of Public Administration (MPA) degree. The professor contended that an MPA degree provides a good education and since the field was still relatively new, it would be easier to gain entrance to an MPA program than to a law school.

Sam was admitted to the first program to which he applied. After sixteen months of diligent effort, Sam had earned his MPA degree. Upon graduation he found a position as an administrative assistant to an older Congressman. Three years later, Sam's boss retired. Sam ran in his place and won by a narrow margin.

Sam's victory illustrates an important point about bouncing back from a blocked route to your goal. Find another door to the same place you want to enter. Don't be dissuaded by people who frown upon an alternate route, considering that route inferior. There is usually more than one path to your goal.

USING THE PROBLEM-SOLVING METHOD TO BOUNCE BACK

Strategies for bouncing back from adversity come in many different forms, as will be described throughout this book. Here we focus on a general approach for coping with adverse circumstances in your life, the problem-solving method. One way or another, when you successfully cope with setback you use some aspect of, or the entire problem-solving method. In essence it involves these steps:

- Clarify the problem (what is the real problem?).
- Find creative alternatives (what options are open?).
- Weigh the alternatives (what are the pros and cons of each alternative?).
- Make a choice (if you want to solve problems you must make tough decisions at some point).
- Develop an action plan and implement (What steps must be taken to get out of this mess?).
- Evaluate outcomes (Did your bounce-back plan work or will you have to try another alternative?).

If the six case histories were presented in more detail, you would discover that each person used some aspect of the problem-solving method. It will suffice here to highlight the key aspect of the problem-solving method used by each of the six people who bounced back.

Tony, the loving husband dumped by his wife, gradually accepted the alternative of becoming a well-adjusted, separated father. He even took the first step toward building a new social life for himself (a realistic action plan).

Gwen, the evicted restaurant owner, deftly surveyed the options available to her and decided to join corporate life. Her story was a clear case of using the problem-solving method.

Wendell, the hunting-accident victim, evaluated the alternatives open to a newly blinded person of his age. He wisely chose to take advantage of all the educational opportunities open to him.

Alex, the injured carpenter, investigated rehabilitation strategies and decided to invent his own technique. His unique plan of entering contests aided both his physical injury and his mental health.

Bob, the firefighter, made computer-like use of the problem-solving method. In a life or death struggle, he chose to remain calm—an alternative that saved his life.

Sam, the man who was determined to become a congressman searched for a creative way of reaching his goal. He knew he had made the right choice only after he achieved his dream goal several years later.

More than one hundred strategies for handling setback are presented throughout the rest of this book. Although not specifically labeled, each one of them fits somewhere into the six-step problem-solving method. After all, if you do not regard adversity as a problem to be solved, what hope is there for resolution? Even praying for help indicates that you have selected one option. Several of the basic coping strategies, such as finding emotional support from others and setting realistic goals, will be mentioned in connection with more than one kind of problem.

DO YOU BOUNCE BACK
OR DO YOU RECOVER?

By now you are probably saying to yourself, "The last time I overcame a serious problem, it took me a long time to recover. It was a gradual process. I certainly didn't bounce back like a punching bag after being struck, or like a millionaire after a $100 loss." How true. Bouncing back from adversity is an ideal situation. For most people, handling setback is a gradual, step-by-step process. Most people rarely bounce back fully from tragedy. Generally, people fumble along and learn to accept change, however painful. Yet the ideal of bouncing back has merit. It points to an uplifting process in life and a spirit of optimism. You can learn to bounce back from non-tragic setbacks, such as everyday annoyances.

If you're wondering about your potential for bouncing back from adversity (or recovering from emotional and physical wounds) turn the page and answer carefully the questionnaire.

NOTES

1. Case history researched by Joe Baldesweiler.
2. Case history researched by Diane Love.
3. Case history based on information in Bill Beeney, "A $24,000 Car—Now That's Some Therapy," *Rochester Democrat and Chronicle,* September 28, 1978, p. 1C. Information updated by interview conducted by present author.
4. Case history researched by Joe Wegman.
5. Case history researched by Craig R. Avery.

chapter two
TEST YOUR RESILIENCY

People differ considerable in their ability to bounce back from setback. Some people seem remarkably resilient, while others seem to crumble when faced with minor disappointment and frustration. Most people fall somewhere in between these two extremes. I have constructed a 50-item questionnaire to help you measure your resiliency—the degree to which you are able to bounce back from adversity. Every question contained in the *Personal Resiliency Questionnaire* relates to some meaningful facet of a person's ability to cope with setback. The more candid you are in filling out this form, the more accurately you will be able to measure your current capacity to cope with trying situations.

An important disclaimer is in order. How well you rebound from hard times relates to many things in your life. Among these factors are the cash value of your liquid assets, the extent to which you are loved and supported by friends and family, your job-related skills and the strength of your personality. The following test is simply an approximate measure of your personal resiliency. It is based on your own evaluations of how you handle some specific incidents or your stance on a particular issue. The test results therefore could be biased toward you if your self-evaluation is too positive. If you self-evaluation is too negative, the results could be biased against you.

THE PERSONAL RESILIENCY QUESTIONNAIRE

Directions: Answer each of the following statements *mostly agree* or *mostly disagree* as it applies to yourself. We are looking for general trends; do not be concerned if you are uncertain as to whether you answer mostly agree or mostly disagree to any one particular question. In taking a questionnaire such as this, it can always be argued that the true answer to any one particular statement is, "It depends on the situation." Despite the validity of this observation, we want you to do your best to indicate whether you would generally agree or disagree with each statement.

In answering each question, assume that you are taking this questionnaire with the intent of learning something about yourself. Only you will see the results. Do not assume you are taking this questionnaire as part of the screening process for a job you want.

		MOSTLY AGREE	MOSTLY DISAGREE	SCORE (see key)
1.	Winning is everything.	☐	☐	____
2.	I'm basically a lucky person.	☐	☐	____
3.	If I have a bad day at work (or school) it tends to ruin my evening.	☐	☐	____
4.	A team that finishes last for two consecutive years should quit the league.	☐	☐	____
5.	I enjoy rainy days because they are always followed by sunshine.	☐	☐	____
6.	If somebody hung up the phone on me, I would stay angry with that person for a long time.	☐	☐	____
7.	If a car splashes me with mud, it only bothers me for a few minutes.	☐	☐	____

14

	MOSTLY AGREE	MOSTLY DISAGREE	SCORE (see key)
8. If I just keep trying, I will get my share of good breaks.	☐	☐	____
9. When there's a flu epidemic going around, I'm one of the first people to catch it.	☐	☐	____
10. If it weren't for a few bad breaks I've received, I'd be much further along in my career.	☐	☐	____
11. There is no disgrace in losing.	☐	☐	____
12. I'm a generally self-confident person.	☐	☐	____
13. Finishing last beats not competing at all.	☐	☐	____
14. I like to take big chances.	☐	☐	____
15. I would feel humiliated if I lost one week's pay on a stock investment.	☐	☐	____
16. I would rather not invite somebody to a party if I thought there was any chance that the person would say no.	☐	☐	____
17. If I want to be a home run hitter, I know I will strike out once in a while.	☐	☐	____
18. I'm a sore loser.	☐	☐	____
19. After a vacation, I need a day to unwind before returning to work.	☐	☐	____
20. Every "no" I encounter is one step closer to a "yes."	☐	☐	____
21. I doubt I could stand the shame of being fired.	☐	☐	____
22. I would be crushed if somebody I loved turned down my marriage proposal.	☐	☐	____

	MOSTLY AGREE	MOSTLY DISAGREE	SCORE (see key)
23. I dwell over mistakes I have made in the past.	☐	☐	____
24. I recover very quickly from a cold.	☐	☐	____
25. I find many days very discouraging.	☐	☐	____
26. The prospects of being heavily in debt frightens me.	☐	☐	____
27. I find it easy to form new personal relationships.	☐	☐	____
28. I think it's a good idea to avoid high risk jobs.	☐	☐	____
29. If I've had a bad weekend, I find it difficult to concentrate on my work on Monday.	☐	☐	____
30. I sometimes wonder if I'll ever get out of debt.	☐	☐	____
31. I have experienced defeat several times in my life.	☐	☐	____
32. I take insults very personally.	☐	☐	____
33. If I ran for political office and were defeated, I would be willing to run again.	☐	☐	____
34. Losing my keys can keep me upset for a week.	☐	☐	____
35. I've gotten to the point where I just don't seem to care about most things.	☐	☐	____
36. The prospects of failing to accomplish something important makes me shudder.	☐	☐	____
37. The last time I was rejected for a job I wanted, it had no particular impact on me.	☐	☐	____
38. It's better to collect unemployment insurance than to waste my			

	MOSTLY AGREE	MOSTLY DISAGREE	SCORE (see key)
time looking for a job in the middle of a recession.	☐	☐	___
39. I very rarely worry about what happened to me yesterday.	☐	☐	___
40. It takes a lot to get me discouraged.	☐	☐	___
41. If two consecutive banks turned down my application for a personal loan, I would forget about borrowing money for the time being.	☐	☐	___
42. I need better than an even chance of success before I risk investing my time in something.	☐	☐	___
43. I look for revenge if I've been voted down on anything.	☐	☐	___
44. It's a wise person who knows when to give up.	☐	☐	___
45. Catastrophies reported in the news make it difficult for me to concentrate on my work.	☐	☐	___
46. If I lost a favorite pet, it would take me at least a year to fully recover.	☐	☐	___
47. I get more than my share of good breaks.	☐	☐	___
48. I hold a grudge for a long time.	☐	☐	___
49. Fate has been unkind to me.	☐	☐	___
50. I enjoy being the underdog once in a while.	☐	☐	___
		Total Score	___

Scoring Your Responses: Give yourself one point as indicated for each statement that you responded to in agreement with the answer key. If your response does not agree with the key, give yourself a zero. Mark down your score in the third column to the right of each question.

Add your points for the 50 statements to arrive at your total score. Note that the term *correct* response is not used. Whether a response is correct or not is a question of personal values and preferences. Each statement that receives one point shows a tendency toward being a resilient person. The scoring key is as follows:

STATEMENT NUMBER	RESILIENT RESPONSE	SCORE
1	Mostly Disagree	1
2	Mostly Agree	1
3	Mostly Disagree	1
4	Mostly Disagree	1
5	Mostly Agree	1
6	Mostly Disagree	1
7	Mostly Agree	1
8	Mostly Agree	1
9	Mostly Disagree	1
10	Mostly Disagree	1
11	Mostly Agree	1
12	Mostly Agree	1
13	Mostly Agree	1
14	Mostly Agree	1
15	Mostly Disagree	1
16	Mostly Disagree	1
17	Mostly Agree	1
18	Mostly Disagree	1
19	Mostly Disagree	1
20	Mostly Agree	1
21	Mostly Disagree	1
22	Mostly Disagree	1
23	Mostly Disagree	1
24	Mostly Agree	1
25	Mostly Disagree	1
26	Mostly Disagree	1
27	Mostly Agree	1
28	Mostly Agree	1
29	Mostly Disagree	1

STATEMENT NUMBER	RESILIENT RESPONSE	SCORE
30	Mostly Disagree	1
31	Mostly Disagree	1
32	Mostly Disagree	1
33	Mostly Agree	1
34	Mostly Disagree	1
35	Mostly Disagree	1
36	Mostly Disagree	1
37	Mostly Agree	1
38	Mostly Disagree	1
39	Mostly Agree	1
40	Mostly Agree	1
41	Mostly Disagree	1
42	Mostly Disagree	1
43	Mostly Disagree	1
44	Mostly Disagree	1
45	Mostly Disagree	1
46	Mostly Disagree	1
47	Mostly Agree	1
48	Mostly Disagree	1
49	Mostly Disagree	1
50	Mostly Agree	1

Interpretation: Your total score on the Personal Resiliency Questionnaire (PRQ) provides you a rough index of your overall tendencies toward being able to bounce back from adversity. The higher your score, the more resilient you are in handling dissappointment, personal trauma, and frustration. The lower your score, the more inclined you are toward having difficulty coping with adversity. As with most questionnaires of this nature, the most extreme scores are usually the most meaningful. For convenience of interpretation, total scores can be placed in one of three categories: *Very Resilient, Moderately Resilient,* and *Not Very Resilient.*

One note of caution: if you score at the very top of this questionnaire (perhaps 46 or higher) you might be too resilient. You may not take setbacks seriously enough and may not learn from your mistakes. It is akin to being too self-confident. If things go wrong, you think other people goofed, not you! Suppose as a top scorer on the PRQ, you are turned down in three consecutive job interviews. Instead of reflecting on what you were doing wrong in the interview, you may simply say, "That's the breaks. I can't help it if three straight interviewers have poor judgment."

Very Resilient. If you scored 41 or more points on the PRQ, you are remarkably effective in bouncing back from setback. When things go very poorly for you, it hurts, but not for long. People in the very resilient category are generally emotionally mature and enthusiastic.

Recent thinking suggests that people in the very resilient category succeed in life because of their Positive Mental Attitude.[1] No matter how bleak things look, they maintain an optimistic inner spirit that helps them surmount obstacles. People in this category virtually refuse to acknowledge defeat. To them, defeats are merely temporary setbacks.

Moderately Resilient. If your total score lies between 11 and 40, you are placed in the moderately resilient category. Most people are moderately resilient. You bounce back readily when faced with some types of adversity. You are much slower to bounce back when faced with other types of adversity. One woman who scored 25 on this questionnaire confesses, "Finding out that I'm overdrawn at the bank throws me for a loop. Being told I have a lousy singing voice puts a black cloud over my head that won't seem to go away. Yet when I was laid off last year, I simply took the bull by the horns and found a new job. It didn't take me long at all. I pleasantly surprised myself."

You might use the PRQ as a checklist for reviewing how you handle various setbacks. For instance, a moderately resilient person might agree with statement 24, "I recover very quickly from a cold." Yet that same individual might agree with statement 32, "I take insults very personally." A person of moderate resiliency can find dozens of strategies and techniques in this book that could prove to be of personal benefit.

Not Very Resilient. If you scored 10 points or lower on the PRQ, you are the type of individual who is bowled over rather easily by adversity, disappointment, and setback. You tend to take reversals too seriously and are very slow to get back up on your feet once tripped. You may give up too early despite the fact that if you held on just a little longer, you would have attained your goal. It's hard for you to emotionally accept the cliche, "Victory is just around the corner." Instead you believe, "Get out while the getting is good."

There is certainly no disgrace in having trouble coping with set-back. By pondering over the experiences of people reported on in this book and taking the recommended strategies seriously, you can improve your ability to rebound from adversity. Your attitude will change; you will become confident about your capacity to bounce back. Equally important, you will pick up dozens of specific tips on how other people facing similar circumstances have rebounded. At a bare minimum, you might question your present methods of dealing with difficult circumstances.

A good starting point in learning more about handling adversity is to examine some strategies for dealing with everyday annoyances.

NOTES

1. W. Clement Stone appears to be the person specifically responsible for developing this idea. Every issue of *Success* Magazine has some information about the value of a Positive Mental Attitude.

chapter three
HANDLING EVERYDAY ANNOYANCES

"Do you know what happened to me today?" said Rudy to his fellow worker. "Some idiot splashed mud and slush all over me just as I was about to cross the street. You should have seen the guy zip past me like he was trying to catch a plane. No regard for other people. The icy slush went through my clothes and stuck to my skin. If I had caught the bastard I would've killed him. My whole day is ruined. Mondays are bad enough as it is."

Poor Rudy, his day, maybe even his week, is ruined (and undoubtedly his job performance for that period) because he was splashed with mud and slush. Rudy is temporarily paralyzed. In his eyes, nothing else is as important as his unfortunate incident, not even a national crisis or his daily tasks. Rudy has succumbed to an everyday annoyance. Many other people act in a manner similar to Rudy. Unfortunately for them, they are overwhelmed by everyday annoyances. This chapter will describe several tactics and attitudes you can use to prevent relatively inconsequential setbacks from getting the best of you.

PLACE THINGS IN PROPER PERSPECTIVE

Have you ever noticed how successful people react maturely when it comes to petty annoyances? They simply shrug off many of those trivial problems that bother people of smaller mental stature. One of the many underlying reasons that these people are successful is that they place things in proper perspective. Some things just are not worth the emotional energy involved in taking them seriously. If a potentially upsetting experience will have no real impact on your life, try to dismiss it with no further thought.

Andrea's situation is a case in point. She was doing so well as a free-lance communications consultant that she decided to purchase her own townhouse. Her boyfriend, Lou, helped Andrea on moving day. As the movers maneuvered Andrea's furniture up the narrow stairwell, Lou watched intently. At one point he noticed that the movers brushed a book case against the edge of a handrailing. The result was a five-inch long scratch, enough to enrage Lou. He urged Andrea to demand reparations from the moving company. "Don't let them get away with this," he exhorted.

Andrea had a different perspective on the gouge. Calmly, she informed Lou, "The movers have been working for two-and-a-half hours. If that's all the damage they do in that period of time, I consider myself lucky. A little wax and two minutes of elbow grease should do the trick. Once everything is moved into place, I'll need to polish the furniture anyway. It's not worth my time agonizing over a little scratch."

Lou was disappointed momentarily that his suggestion was rebuffed. But he did receive a flash of insight about the value of shrugging off a minor problem—why make moving day any more harassing than it already is?

"Place Things in Proper Perspective" is a psychological tactic. Perspective building is a method of coping with adversity that has many different applications.

WRITE IT OFF

Early in my career, I participated in evaluating an executive for a key position. The job candidate in question was a California resident who was being considered for a vice-presidential position with a firm headquartered in New York. Negotiations continued for a month. During the process of considering the post, the candidate made two trips to New York. His wife was included on one of these trips. The New York firm paid the full tab, including travel expenses for the candidate's wife.

Finally the candidate was extended an offer which he accepted. One week later he called the firm to explain that he had changed his mind, citing that he did not desire to move. Concerned that I had encouraged the firm to pursue the executive who turned down the offer, extended my apologies for the waste of time and money. Seemingly unperturbed, the company president told me, "Sure it would have been nice if things worked out. But don't worry, we'll simply write off the expense and continue our search for the right person."

Few of us have the resources of a large corporation, but we do have the wherewithal to write off minor annoyances. The strategy is to dismiss the minor setback as an inevitable part of daily living. No life proceeds without a few minor reversals, so a few losses have to be absorbed. Bud's situation illustrates the proper mental set for writing off minor losses.

One Saturday, Bud and his teenage daughter, Mimi, embarked on a bike hike to the next town. Included in their gear was a packed picnic basket. For Bud and Mimi, this was a special day because they dearly loved to spend some quiet time together. At lunchtime, they enjoyed a roadside picnic. The Virginia hillside at which they ate lunch was so lovely that Bud decided to shoot a few pictures with his 35mm camera. Mimi, his favorite model, obliged. After an hour of picture taking and picnicking the two proceeded on their journey.

Pleasantly fatigued, Bud and Mimi returned home late that afternoon. As Bud began to describe the events of the day to his wife, he blurted out, "Come to think of it, I left my flash attachment behind. We stopped to shoot some pictures. I set the flash down near the rock where Mimi was posing. I would be very hard to figure out exactly where we left it."

"I'm so sorry," said Mimi. "It was partly my fault. I should have watched more closely. Maybe a friend of mine and I can bike back there tomorrow." Bud's wife piped in, "That makes it a very expensive bicycle trip. You should be more careful."

Rather than allowing the lost flash attachment cancel out the pleasures derived from his outing, Bud rationalized the loss in his mind. He told his wife and daughter:

Don't worry about it. I can't deny it was an expensive bicycle trip, but don't place all the blame on this one trip. It's October now and the only things I've lost all year are an old sweater and the flash attachment. That's about fifty dollars worth of losses for ten months. Our fuel bill for air conditioning exceeds that figure five months a year. Fifty dollars is a pretty small loss. Especially when you look at it as a percentage of my $25,000 a year income. Just put that in the small loss column.

Why don't you take the lead from Bud's arithmetic logic? Just divide your next small loss by your total income and see if the answer warrants an emotional upheaval on your part.

"Write It Off" is akin to placing things in proper perspective. It is also a form of realistic decision making. You prevent further losses in an adverse situation by refusing to agonize over the losses you have already incurred.

GRIT YOUR TEETH

Gritting your teeth is a useful and readily available strategy for dealing with everyday annoyances. If done to excess, it is a maladaptive way of coping with frustration. A dentist I know is convinced that he can find out a lot about a patient's employer through a dental examination. In his words, "If a patient has severely ground-down teeth, it usually means that the individual works for a high pressure outfit. If a person's teeth are not ground down, it usually means they work in a less hectic environment." Thus, literally gritting your teeth in response to stress can have adverse physical consequences.

Gritting your teeth over big problems in the long run is certainly not a constructive solution to your problems. Yet it can help you deal with a large number of relatively minor problems that will probably pass away quickly on their own. Here's a tentative list of everyday annoyances that readily can be handled by gritting your teeth and not letting things get you down:

- Leaving for work in the morning, you decide to empty the garbage. A few seconds after picking up the bag of garbage, you discover it is wet and sloppy. While pondering what to do, the bag breaks and a mixture of coffee grinds, egg shells and other debris spill over your shoes.

- You sit down quickly in an easy chair and discover instantly that you left a ballpoint pen in your backpocket. The ink leaves a blue stain on your jeans, your legs, and the easy chair.
- The light bulb in your reading lamp burns out. After several minutes of searching, you find a replacement. While trying to screw in the bulb, you drop it on the floor and it shatters.
- While trying to find change to give to a toll booth attendant, you slam your hand into your steering wheel, breaking the nail on your index finger.
- You step out the front door ten minutes before the first dinner guest is scheduled to arrive. As you glance at the doormat, you discover that your cat has deposited a decapitated chipmunk in front of the door.

"Grit Your Teeth" is related to the idea that a person accepts some pain and displeasure as inevitable in life. Following this reality principle, you absorb a little pain, knowing that larger pleasures will be forthcoming.

DIVERT YOUR IMPATIENCE

A major daily source of duress is waiting on lines. Among the most patience-testing situations are standing in line at the bank, sitting in a car while waiting for a traffic artery to unclog, and waiting your turn to be checked out in a supermarket. Many otherwise mature individuals find their days ruined by their negative attitude toward waiting in line. This last sentence should be carefully analyzed. Notice that I stressed, their negative attitude. It is your perception of the situation that causes the problem.

Being stuck on a line is a classic source of frustration. The goal you want to achieve—getting your business conducted, or arriving at your destination—is blocked. One solution is to visit banks, supermarkets, and drive on highways when the traffic is light. Since most people do not have a sufficiently flexible work schedule to exercise that alternative, another solution must be found. An antidote of proven effectiveness is to find some constructive activity to accomplish while waiting. When waiting time is converted into useful time, the sense of frustration dissipates. Buzzy, a life insurance sales representative and estate planner, describes his use of waiting time:

> Since I'm a real go-getter, I used to get irritated when I had to wait in line. I read a book about time management that gave me a potent hint about dealing with the problem. Now, if I am on a long line, I whip out my notebook and work on my activity list for the day or week. My waiting-in-line time has become my planning time. When I tell other people about my method, they usually contend I'll get in a traffic accident that way. In a car, I use a slightly different approach. I dictate some of my ideas about a tough case on which I might be working; during the week, I will listen to these cassettes in my den or office. It would be fair to say that making good use of waiting time has led me to thousands of dollars in new business. They say in my business, "the person who fails to plan, plans to fail," and it's true.

Not everybody can convert waiting time into dollars, but you can lower your annoyance level by finding something constructive to do with that time. Small useful activities such as cleaning out your wallet, polishing your eyeglasses, and reading the newspaper can be accomplished during waiting-in-line time.

"Divert Your Impatience" is a variation of the defense mechanism known as *displacement.* Typical displacement is for you to displace anger or hostility on to somebody else. If you are abused by your boss, you abuse your spouse or lover. To be successful, you displace (divert) a negative feeling (impatience) into a constructive activity such as short-range planning.

BE PERSISTENT

A universally applicable strategy for handling adversity is to be persistent. Being persistent is useful in handling both big and small problems. Many daily sources of irritation only can be overcome by a diligent reapplication of your efforts. Part of the frustration is that you have to run the same errand several times. Trying to get a leaky automobile radiator repaired properly falls into this category. Upon bringing the car home from the repair shop, it appears that the baffling problem has been conquered. So often within a few days, the year-around coolant once again begins to form puddles under your car. Your only recourse is to trundle off to the repair shop again, hoping that this time the antidote will stick. If you can stomach a third trip, the problem will usually be conquered. Leaky radiators are not easy to fix, however well-intended the mechanic.

Persistence can be an essential virtue in coping with the everyday annoyances sometimes created by a bureaucracy. An objective point of view usually reveals that a bureaucracy is not out to get you. What has happened, however, is that a complex chain of command combined with an abundance of rules and regulations creates harrassment. Here is how Tony, a frequent business traveller, used persistance to overcome an annoying predicament:

As usual, I phoned in my airline reservation for a flight between Cleveland and Chicago. Since it was a popular flight, I made the call a month early. One week before my scheduled departure date, I realized that the tickets had not yet arrived at my house and called the airline. They explained that the reason I had not been sent the tickets was that they had not been billed to my credit card number. Because of this clerical error the tickets were not placed in the mail.

I then asked what I should do about getting the tickets. They told me they would hold the tickets up to forty-five minutes before flight time. I figured that since I was taking the six A.M. flight, it would be very difficult to get to the airport over forty-five minutes before flight time. So I made a special trip to the airport one day prior to my departure date to pick up the tickets.

I explained the problem to the reservation clerk. She told me that the airline had been having trouble lately because of new help. I was glad to have the issue finally settled, even if it meant a special trip to the airport. As it worked out I was glad too soon.

Two weeks later I received my monthly bank credit-card bill. I was billed for two roundtrip flights for the Chicago trip. Somehow the computer received two sets of identical instructions. My anger was building up, particularly since I would now be charged interest on double the amount I really owed.

I called the airline reservation department to explain what happened. As usual, it took a few minutes before I could get beyond a recorded voice. The woman who finally took my call told me to call back the next day when there would be somebody on duty who could help me.

I followed her instructions and went into my pitch the next day. This time a man answered at the airlines. He told me there was no local jurisdiction over billing problems. I was told to send my airline reservation ticket receipts to an address in the far west. I explained that I had already submitted by receipts to my company for expense account purposes.

Next, I sent a photocopy of the bank credit-card bill to the airline central credit office. Three weeks later they sent me an affidavit to sign. I had to swear that I never received the missing tickets. Two credit card statements later, the duplicate charge had finally been removed. I had probably been charged two months unnecessary interest. At that point I didn't care. I kept trying and I finally won. I guess it's all part of living in the computer age.

Tony handled this situation rather well. He persisted in winning his victory without losing total emotional control. He could swear to never using that airline again, but that would be self-defeating because they schedule flights to places he needs to visit at the times he wants to travel. He could pursue the small unjust interest charge, but the rewards would hardly be worth the effort. Tony claims he is no longer bothered by the incident.

"Be Persistent" is a straightforward application of goal-oriented activity. The living organism—from white rat to supreme court justice—keeps on repeating the behavior that will lead to goal attainment. Persistence remains a highly useful method of coping with adversity.

RISE ABOVE IT

Jim, a married man with four children, was a successful middle manager in an insurance company. To outsiders, his marriage seemed stable. Jim took a keen interest in his four children and valued his marriage. However, Jim was not opposed to an occasional dalliance. One night after a dinner meeting in a downtown hotel, Jim found himself in the mood for some adventure. A woman standing outside the hotel beckoned to Jim. Without thinking, Jim asked the apparent prostitute, "How much and what do I get for my money?"

As soon as Jim agreed to a seventy-five dollar fee, the attractive woman replied, "I'm a police officer and you're under arrest." Jim spent one night in jail, paid his fine, and was released from custody. Unfortunately, Jim was not released from publicity and embarrassment. His name was included in the morning paper among a long list of other would-be Johns entrapped by police workers.

Jim's wife was upset, two of his children were depressed, one was angry, and the oldest one amused. At work, Jim could feel the tension among his superiors and subordinates. A good friend of Jim's employed by the same company told Jim that the rumors were getting vicious.

Jim's strategy was not to run and hide but to rise above gossip. In dealings with his co-workers and subordinates, Jim smiled and went about business as usual. He expressed his apologies to his immediate superiors and assured them that this was a one-time incident that had no bearing upon his job performance. Within three weeks, things were back to normal (at least on the job).

You may take issue with Jim's morality, but his strategy of coping with annoying gossip was sound. Instead of quitting his job—thereby making a major life issue out of his indiscretion—Jim simply rose above the snickering of others. If this issue led to a breakup of Jim's marriage or a career setback (neither of which happened) you would not consider his encounter with the policewoman an everyday annoyance. Gossip, however, is usually best treated as an everyday annoyance. Rise above it and it will go away.

"Rise above it" is a healthy form of the defense mechanism called *denial*. Ignore something in your mind and it will sometimes disappear.

TAKE ONE DAY AT A TIME

Jan wondered if she would ever survive the month of January. She and her two sons had lived as a threesome since her husband left the state a couple of years earlier. Jan and the children worked together as a team to keep the home situation running smoothly. Each boy did his share of household chores and chipped in with the tasks the father used to perform, such as chopping wood for the woodburning stove.

During January, Jan and her children ran afoul of good fortune. One particular evening, when the temperature dropped to ten below zero, the wallboard in back of the stove began to smolder. The boys threw water on it just in time to prevent a major fire. Jan kept the stove temperature as low as feasible until the stove could be relocated further from the wall. Two days later, a warm spell settled in, creating a massive formation of icicles on the edge of their roof. One of the gutters caved in, straining Jan's repair budget further.

The following week, Jan and the boys went to a public park for a morning of cross country skiing. Returning to their car at noon, Jan discovered that she had lost her keys. Since finding lost keys over three miles of ski trails seemed impossible, Jan and the boys hitched back to the town. It took Jan until late Sunday afternoon to get a ride back to the car with the spare keys in hand. By then, the car battery had gone dead. A benevolent stranger gave Jan a booster start. Since no automotive discount stores were open that Sunday, Jan was forced to pay a premium price for a replacement battery at a service station.

As the middle of the month approached, things seemed to go better for Jan and the boys. The outlook, however, quickly reverted to gloom. In sequence, all three came down with the Hong Kong flu. As soon as they recouperated, the boys received a letter from their father that he would be unable to invite them to his home for a February weekend as planned. Both boys were bitterly disappointed.

The important message to remember is that Jan did not fall apart under the barrage of all these minor annoyances. In her words:

> I just took each day one at a time. My story sounds so bad, yet no real catastrophe happened to us. I felt like a fool losing my keys in the snow. The bad news about the woodburning stove was really good news. The near disaster alerted us to have the stove properly installed. The boys wound up visiting their father in March. So they were disappointed for a month, but not forever.
>
> As the trickle of bad news poured in, it began to get me sort of giddy. One night at the dinner table the boys and I went into hysterics rehashing all the zany things that had happened to us in a

couple of weeks. As bad as the events of the month of January were they helped me to develop an attitude that has stuck with me ever since. I'll deal with each day's vexing problem on its own merit. I don't try to link one day's bad news with yesterday's bad news. Each day is its own separate challenge.

"Take One Day at a Time" is closely tied in with goal theory. Sometimes setting easy-to-reach goals helps you rebuild your self-confidence. Thus instead of planning to make big improvements all at once, tackle each day's most vexing problem as it arises.

THIS, TOO, WILL PASS

If you can intellectually and emotionally accept the fact that almost all uncomfortable situations eventually run their course, you will bounce back with great alacrity. Handling issues of minor consequence will be made easier when you realize that things will pass in time. Phil, a college student, used this attitude to help him deal with a situation that viewed in another light might have been oppressive.[1]

As an accounting major, I expected that any work-study job I took would be closely related to professional accounting. My college lined me up a job as an assistant bookkeeper to give me some actual work experience. I will admit I did some actual bookkeeping work but the majority of the time I ran errands, plotted graphs for another firm that rented space in the same building, typed invoices, and other menial jobs. I didn't expect to be running the place, but I was looking forward to higher level work. It was kind of frustrating, and at times boring. It didn't seem as if you needed college training to do those kind of tasks.

Since my work-study program lasted only eleven weeks, coping with the problem wasn't too hard. I just kept thinking that I wasn't going to be doing this type of work for the rest of my working days. I looked at the calendar each week to remind myself that I would soon be back in a college classroom learning more about accounting. Recognizing that the worst would soon be over helped me appreciate the fact that I was moving forward in my field, even if the steps seemed small.

Phil imparts an important message to us all. Many annoying circumstances have a natural life cycle with a beginning, middle, and end.
Enduring these annoyances often fits into a larger puzzle with a beneficial result.

"This, Too, Will Pass" might be considered an example of rational
problem solving. You can choose to do nothing as one of the
alternatives. Since the adverse situation will go away on its own,
you do nothing.

LET GOOD NEWS HELP

Good news has a magical way of diminishing the impact of irritations
and annoyances. Have you ever had an ailing back temporarily cured
by the good news of receiving an unexpected check in the mail? Or
have your cold symptoms suddenly disappeared when you find out that
somebody you didn't think cared about you suddenly tells you how
much he or she appreciates you?

An illustration of good news eradicating an annoying condition
involves Bill, a Little League baseball coach. Bill was under his car one
evening trying to determine the cause of a clicking sound that occurred
whenever the car exceeded about twenty miles per hour. Bill didn't
locate the source of the problem, but he did succeed in pinching a
nerve in the back of his neck while maneuvering under the car.

The antidote offered by Bill's orthopedic surgeon was for him to
wear a large cumbersome collar. It made Bill look as if he had recently
broken his neck. By the third day of wearing his neck brace (a large
white collar) Bill tired of explaining the nature of his injury to others.
Bill's discomfort multiplied when he had to attend little league practice
in oppresive heat. Soon he began to envision maggots under his collar,
hardly an everyday annoyance despite the general subject of this chapter. Bill thought of wearing a scarf over his collar, but decided that such
a disguise in the middle of the summer would elicit more commentary
than a neck collar.

Coach Bill sweated out one more practice, preparing his team for
Saturday morning's big game against the heavily favored horde of

eight-year olds sponsored by Dunkin Donuts. On Saturday morning, Bill's delight, his Gladstone Chevrolet Raiders beat the Dunkin Donut Gladiators, 27 to 18.

Bill's wife rushed up to congratulate him. First, however, she sympathetically asked, "Honey, how is the pain in your neck?" Bill honestly responded, "What pain? Our team won."

Perhaps you too can use your next bit of good news to ease the pain of your most pressing everyday annoyance. The phenomenon might be more than psychological. Positive emotion is said to release a hormone called endorphin which is a natural painkiller. Since endorphin is not commercially available, you have to generate your own through good news or some other exhilarating experience.

"Let Good News Help" boils down to allowing yourself the advantages of *eustress,* a positive form of stress that leads to healthy consequences such as creative thinking and pain reduction.

NOTES

1. Mike Scarcelli researched this incident.

chapter four
HANDLING CRITICISM AND REJECTION

The reason I'm so abrasive with people is that I try to reject them before they reject me.

Being criticized by my boss is about as much fun as being kicked in the stomach by my horse.

Every semester when I get those student evaluations, I get an awful nervous feeling inside my body. If I come across a very negative comment, I usually have to run to the bathroom.

When I'm criticized, I usually thank the person who offered it to me. Criticism has been one of my best methods of learning to become a more effective sales rep.

The honest comments above made by four different people tell us a lot about the nature of criticism and rejection. Both can hurt, but they can also help a person. Part of the master plan for bouncing back from adversity is to be able to handle criticism and rejection. Most setbacks in life involve some element of criticism and rejection. The twelve strategies and attitudes described in the following pages are designed to help you cope with these potentially disruptive forces. Let's look at a basic fact about rejection and criticism.

REMEMBER THAT REJECTION AND CRITICISM ARE INEVITABLE

In personal life as well as on the job, everybody is subject to some criticism and rejection. The more complex and demanding your life, the greater the chance that you will be criticized and rejected. Put in another perspective, the more visible you are the more likely it is that somebody will reject or criticize you.

People will find you not to their liking (which is ordinarily interpreted as rejection) for a variety of reasons that do not detract from your worth as an individual. As an informal experiment along these lines, I asked a group of college women how they might like to develop a relationship with Dr. Carl Sagan, the famous astronomer, science writer, and star of television's "Cosmos." We made the assumption that Dr. Sagan was unattached at the time. As you would expect, most of the women who were familiar with the famous astronomer expressed a positive reaction. One woman admitted that she was virtually in love with Dr. Sagan. But there were plenty of rejecting statements. Among them: "I don't care who he is, I would never date a middle-age man." "The guy is too theoretical for me." "No good. He's too conceited." "Not for me. I don't like the way he got rid of his first wife."

Any job with substantial public contact involves considerable criticism and rejection. If you try to accept this notion beforehand, it will ease the potential sting of being criticized or rejected by the people you are trying to help. Ralph, the owner and president of a small company that manufactures electric switches, describes how he handles criticism:

> I often tell my wife in a joking way that maybe I should resign and take a lesser job in my own firm. There's a myth circulating that all company owners are millionaires and life is a piece of cake for them. What the public doesn't realize is all the gaff the owner takes. The government tells us what we're doing wrong from a safety standpoint and a tax standpoint. Some of our customers want to channel their complaints to me only. It doesn't matter who made the mistake, I'm their official complaint department.
>
> I may be the president, but that doesn't stop some of our younger employees from telling me how to run the business. Right now we're going through a union campaign and I've received a lot of criticism from the organizers. They thought nothing of printing up

courageous to solicit the criticism. An additional advantage of asking for criticism is that it helps place any points of contention between you and the criticizer on a problem-solving basis. The two of you are trying to improve a work or personal relationship rather than venting anger. Here are several examples of how a person might ask for feedback, thus receiving some criticism before a real problem develops:

> MAN TO WOMAN: We've been seeing each other for two months now. Is there anything I'm doing that displeases you? Or is there something I should be doing that I'm not doing?

> SALES REPRESENTATIVE TO BOSS: I've been working this territory for six months now. I receive no complaints, but I'm sure I've made some mistakes. Can you offer me any constructive suggestions?

> TAX CONSULTANT TO CLIENT: I sure do appreciate your business year after year. I enjoy preparing your tax forms. Is there anyway I could be serving you better? Is there anything we're doing that you don't like? Your answer is important to me.

"Ask for Feedback" is another aspect of using the problem-solving method. In order to solve your problem, you gather together relevant information. It fits into the category of clarifying the problem.

USE THE FOGGING METHOD

Psychologists have developed a technique specifically designed to help you deal with manipulative criticism.[1] Manipulative criticism is designed to get you to do something another person wants you to do that is not necessarily in your best interests. In fogging, you respond to manipulative criticism as if you were a fog bank. You thus are virtually unaffected by the criticism and will be able to get across your point. The learner of the fogging technique is instructed to offer no resistance to the criticism. You need considerable practice to become adept at fogging. For openers, here are three examples of fogging in action:

> CRITIC: I see that you are sloppy looking as usual.
> PERSON CRITICIZED: That's right, I look the same today as I usually do.

CRITIC: How atrocious! You made five errors in preparing that tax return.

PERSON CRITICIZED: That's true. I counted the errors you've circled in red. There were exactly five.

CRITIC: Have you ever thought of giving up your career as a newspaper reporter to become a beachcomber?

PERSON CRITICIZED: I could see some merit in giving up my career in journalism and becoming a beachcomber.

"Use the Fogging Method" is itself a psychological technique that is part of assertiveness training. Instead of allowing your self-esteem to be lowered by the criticizer, you utilize a technique that allows the criticism to pass right by.

USE NEGATIVE ASSERTION

People tend to feel needlessly guilty when confronted with mistakes. Because of your feelings of guilt (and associated anxiety), you seek forgiveness or deny the error. The antidote is a skill called negative assertion. This skill can help you quickly learn to cope with errors or negative points about you.[2] Using this technique, you take the initiative to criticize yourself, thus stealing the thunder from the criticizer. (This is similar to fogging.) The following examples illustrate negative assertion:

You are out on a date, headed down the highway toward a theatre ten miles away. You reach into your pocket and discover that you have left the tickets behind. Knowing that your date is temperamental, you decide to use a negative assertion to spare the fireworks. You calmly inform your partner "I've really flubbed our evening. The tickets are back home in my desk drawer. Either we forget the play entirely, or we turn around and go back to my place. If we go back, we'll miss most of the first act. If we don't go back, we'll have to do something else this evening. What's your choice?"

In the situation just mentioned you have avoided an altercation with your temperamental partner. The result would have been quite different if you had initially said, "Oops, I forgot the tickets. You forgot to remind me." That approach would have invited a barrage of verbal aggressiveness directed at you.

A second example is when you are invited out to lunch with your boss and an important client. After lunch your boss says to you, "I think you made a bad decision in wearing casual clothes to lunch. Why didn't you wear more businesslike attire? Your clothing just didn't fit the occasion."

Using a negative assertion you respond, "That was poor judgment on my part. I should have known to wear businesslike attire for this important occasion."

Although we recommend fogging and negative assertion as useful methods for handling criticism, they both have a potential drawback. If your responses are overdone, you will come across as a smart aleck and your image and reputation will suffer as a result.

"Use Negative Assertion" is another example of nondefensive behavior. Many people will have trouble using this technique because it provides a temporary assault on your self-esteem. Its value, however, is that criticizing yourself is usually better than allowing somebody else the privilege.

ASK FOR SPECIFIC EXAMPLES (NEGATIVE INQUIRY)

Another mature and constructive way of dealing with criticism launched at you is to ask the criticizer for specific examples of what you are doing wrong.[3] By so doing you behave as if criticism does not bother you. The criticizer does not succeed in belittling you or making you defensive. Instead, you are putting criticsm on a problem-solving plane where it belongs. Another advantage of negative inquiry is that it forces the criticizer to examine what he or she considers right and wrong. In the process of examining these values, the criticizer may come to realize that some of the criticism is without foundation.

Imagine this scenario. Alva announces to her husband, Brad, that she plans to go out to dinner with several of her friends this Friday evening. Brad is upset, but Alva uses negative inquiry to handle the criticism.

ALVA: By the way, Brad, I'll be going out to dinner with a couple of friends this Friday. I assume you can manage things for yourself.

BRAD: I'm not sure I like the idea of you going out on Friday night. Why do you have to go out this Friday?

ALVA:: What don't you like about my going out this Friday?

BRAD: It's just not right for you to take off on Friday night.

ALVA: But what isn't right about it?

BRAD We're a married couple. You shouldn't be going out by yourself.

ALVA: I'm not going out by myself. I'm going out with Doris and Sue. What's wrong with my going out with Doris and Sue?

BRAD: If you go out with Doris and Sue, then I'll be alone on Friday.

ALVA: True, you will be alone if you choose. But what is wrong with your being alone on Friday evening?

BRAD: I guess that if a man is married, he shouldn't have to be alone on Friday evening.

ALVA: It's fine with me if you go out with your friends. Why is that bad for you?

BRAD: To tell you the truth, I would prefer to be with you. I don't think it's right for me not to be with you.

ALVA: What isn't right about it?

BRAD: It makes me feel left out, as if you don't really want to be with me.

ALVA: Please don't interpret it that way. We can be together when I get back. I should be home by ten.

BRAD: I guess you're right. Have a good time.

I can hear some readers muttering these words, "Brad is too good to be true. My spouse would never listen to reason." Nevertheless, if you begin to practice negative inquiry, you will discover that many instances of criticism directed at you will dissipate. In a typical dialogue between the criticizer and criticized, the conflict escalates because the person being criticized becomes defensive and hostile. The criticizer, in turn, becomes more vehement. If the person being critized, however, sincerely asks for examples of errors, the criticizer will be more compassionate. Imagine the following oft-repeated scenario between a secretary and boss:

BOSS: I don't like the way you've been handling my travel reservations lately.

SECRETARY: I'm sorry to hear that. What's wrong?

BOSS: They're messed up.

SECRETARY: Messed up in what way?

BOSS: The last time you booked me on a flight to Los Angeles, I got into town pretty late.

SECRETARY: How late did you arrive in town?

BOSS: Much too late to have a few hours out on the town.

SECRETARY: What else about my travel reservations has been a problem?

BOSS   You put me in the wrong section of town.
SECRETARY: What was wrong with the section of town you stayed at in Los Angeles?
BOSS: It was away from all the excitement. You know, the honky-tonk section where all the fun is.
SECRETARY: Now I understand. You want a night on the town and you want to be near the action. Can you offer me any other suggestions?
BOSS: No, you haven't been doing that bad a job. I guess I didn't give you specific enough suggestions before.

Notice how this secretary used negative inquiry to her advantage. At the end of the interchange, both the secretary and the boss have improved their working relationship. If the secretary had become defensive, the boss would probably have become increasingly critical.

"Ask for Specific Examples (Negative Inquiry)" is also a technique based on the psychological technique of assertiveness training, which itself was originally a method of psychotherapy. Asking for specifics from your criticizer also fits into the problem-solving method of coping with setback. You gather more relevant facts in order to make a sound decision.

LOOK WHO'S TALKING

A bias that people have is that the criticizer is always right. You certainly must learn to profit from constructive feedback, but you also must remember that people criticize you based on their values. Suppose a guest says to you, "My, your house is cold." You check your thermometer; it registers 67°F. From your guest's standpoint, it may be cold, but from an energy conservationist's standpoint, the house temperature is just about right.

The purpose of the strategy of acknowledging who is criticizing is to look beyond the critic's facade.[4] Try to understand why the critic is criticizing you. Is he or she jealous, resentful, or simply well-intended? Perhaps the critic needs to put you down just to feel adequate. Next is a list of criticisms frequently offered to people. Accompanying each one is a possible underlying motive, other than trying to correct a situation that needs correcting.

CRITICISM: I'm worried about how hard you're working. If you don't slow down you might get a heart attack.
POSSIBLE QUESTIONABLE MOTIVE: Criticizer wants you to slow down so you don't make him or her look so bad. If you keep up this pace, you will be the one who earns that top income.

CRITICISM: Don't you think you're investing too much into money market certificates? I've heard it's much better to buy materials rather than save money during a period of high inflation.
POSSIBLE QUESTIONABLE MOTIVE: Criticizer would prefer that you invest your money in something that would benefit him or her directly like a new stereo set or a vacation trip.

CRITICISM: I don't think those jeans look good on you. They're made for somebody much younger than you.
POSSIBLE QUESTIONABLE MOTIVE: I don't want you to look so sexy. Somebody else might notice you and try to begin a relationship with you. That would leave me out in the cold.

"Look Who's Talking" asks you to apply motivational theory to your repertoire of techniques for handling setback. You try to determine why you are being criticized—what is the underlying reason that your critic is sticking it to you! The most basic premise of psychology is that all behavior has a cause.

LOOK FOR THE HIDDEN AGENDA

As previously stated, many forms of criticism have a hidden agenda. The hidden agenda critic says one thing and means another. However, the hidden agenda critic is more aware of the intended criticism than people with questionable motives. For example, the person who criticized the other for wearing tight jeans might not even realize that he or she is concerned about somebody else noticing the person being criticized. The hidden agenda critic is unable or unwilling to criticize directly and therefore chooses the indirect route.

One hidden agenda critic I vividly recall was a college professor who had been contracted by a publisher to criticize a textbook manuscript I was preparing. In rather disparaging tones, the professor criticized me for "insufficient scholarship in citing the more important developments in the field of improving managerial performance." Although this criticism sounds specific, it really wasn't too helpful. I needed a "for instance." My editor agreed to call the professor and ask for a study or two that should have been cited. The critical professor then provided the editor with a reprint of a study he had done which he considered to be an "important development in the field of improving managerial performance." The professor could have saved me a lot of time by telling me directly that I stepped on his intellectual toes by not citing his allegedly monumental work. If he had sent me a copy of his study, I would have gladly mentioned it in my book.

Winning at Work: A Book for Women provides a cogent anecdote about the importance of looking for the hidden agenda in criticism. As reported by its authors,

> Karen worked for a drug rehabilitation program administered by the state government, and her boss was a hidden agenda critic. Part of the program was funded by a federal grant, and for the administrative purpose of keeping the grant, her boss needed to show statistical evidence that a certain number of men were moving from prison to work release. Instead of explaining his dilemma, he criticized Karen. "You've had enough time to get the men ready. Why aren't more of them in work release?" She knew that you don't effect a psychological cure by a time clock, but her boss's insistence, coupled with his inability to communicate the administrative point of view, led both people to make mistakes.[6]

"Look for the Hidden Agenda" asks you to dig for the underlying determinant of behavior. What the person says on the surface may not be the real reason for his or her behavior. A good starting point is using this strategy to ask yourself the needs or points that another person has in taking a particular position.

EXAMINE WHY YOU WERE REJECTED

Rejection is a form of unstated criticism. If you are rejected or ignored, you are being criticized often without the benefit of an explanation. The rejection letter from a prospective employer might state, "Although we consider you a highly qualified candidate, we decided to offer the position to an individual with more experience." This convenient letter could mean almost anything, but it means rejection for you. Sometimes a candid inquiry on your part will reveal the true cause of the rejection. A personnel specialist in the company that did not make you a job offer might tell you informally, "To tell you the truth, we thought your employment record lacked the stability we look for. You seem to be a job hopper."

At other times, a strong dose of self-examination may be necessary to find out why you were rejected. The reasons for rejection in social situations are usually so difficult to obtain that self-examination is the method of choice. Sam, a tennis enthusiast, was having a difficult time joining a foursome for indoor tennis. After repeated invitations for others to rent time with him were rejected, Sam finally went the anonymous route. He posted this notice on his tennis club's board, "Mens, 'A' player seeking to play doubles, any night or weekend day. Call Sam at 424–0842." Sam finally connected with three new club members who desperately needed a fourth for doubles.

Sam began to get a message. The only players who wanted him for a fourth were people who did not know him. In an agonizing session of self-appraisal, Sam came up with four negative facts about his tennis behavior: One, he screamed more than most people when he missed an easy shot. Two, he was usually remiss in taking his turn at bringing new balls. Three, he insisted on wearing clothing to the court more suited for a schoolyard basketball game than a tennis club. Four, he was too critical of his partner when his team was behind in doubles.

Sam's self-appraisal worked; he made a determined effort to shore up his four tennis shortcomings. Sam was so well behaved with his three new partners that they considered themselves lucky to include a refined and stylish player in their foursome.

"Examine Why You Were Rejected" is a direct application of the problem-solving method. You clarify the problem by digging for the facts behind your rejection.

ADJUST YOUR LEVEL OF EXPECTATION

The secret of success in this strategy is lowering your goals, particulary since the true meaning of success is to attain your goals. Consequently, if you are encountering too much rejection and frustration, you might consider adjusting your level of expectation. Perhaps you are simply expecting too much yield from your efforts. A young man from Toronto aspired toward becoming a nationally recognized photographer. He envisioned himself freelancing for major magazines, newspapers, and news services. After two years of rejection he finally developed a more realistic level of expectation. He explains:

> I finally got wise and stopped beating my head against the wall. The important thing is to make a living as a photographer. That's rare enough. Presently, I'm shooting pictures for three suburban newspapers. I also get an occasional magazine assignment. I'll do anything except proms, weddings, and bar mitzvahs. I still want to hit it big someday. But in the meantime, I can proudly say that I'm a professional photographer.

The well-publicized mid-career crisis often manifests itself when a person is bypassed for promotion several times. If a person can modify the level of expectation, the crisis can be resolved.[7] Such is the case for Biff, who worked his way up the factory ladder from a tool-and-die maker to a plant superintendent. Biff's area of responsibility involved several hundred people, including seven supervisors. As Biff approached age 50, he became despondent. He began to withdraw from regular contact with his supervisors, which was unusual for Biff.

Aside from losing contact with his people, Biff became delinquent on many of his written reports to top management. Don, the plant manager, insisted that he and Biff have a long lunch together. "Biff, what's gone wrong?" asked Don in a concerned tone. "What's happened to our best superintendent? You are acting like an Ivy League plant superintendent. Furthermore, why are your reports late? I know we all hate filling out forms, but we've always been able to count on you in the past."

"Don, you've been honest enough to tell me how things really are. I'll return the favor," responded Biff. "All of a sudden things are closing in on me. I've been passed over for promotion twice now. The only thing I see ahead of me is more of the same. I'll be superintendent of this plant until 1997, when it will be time for retirement. I've got a lot of ambition left. It's discouraging when a man realizes he's topped out in a company that's been his whole life."

"Biff," continued Don, "Let me tell you about your future with us as I see it. Every member of management I've spoken to thinks you're a superb superintendent. We wouldn't take three bright young college graduates in an even trade for Biff. Despite all those good things I've said, we don't see you as having potential beyond your present job."

Biff asked with a perplexed expression, "Why not?" "Because," answered Don, "you've got two strikes against you. First of all, you lack a college degree. You can't become a plant manager or a front office executive in our company without a college degree. The second strike is that we see you as a diamond in the rough, a bull-of-the woods type. That approach goes over big out on the shop floor, but it's not suited for the executive suite."

Don and Biff returned from the long lunch on good terms. Biff appreciated being leveled with, and Don appreciated Biff's capacity to accept the truth. Within one week, Don noticed that Biff had returned to his same energetic self. He was back on the shop floor in person-to-person discussions with his supervisors. Biff caught up on his back reports, and his new weekly report was handed in promptly.

Don commented, "It's great to see the true Biff back in stride. What's happened?"

Biff answered, "The evening of our luncheon get-together, I changed my goals. I've decided to become the best superintendent this plant has ever had."

"Adjust Your Level of Expectation" fits into goal theory. When you establish realistic (sensible) goals you are likely to reach them and therefore increase your level of satisfaction. If you reach your first realistic goal, then stretch yourself a little more on the next go-around.

REMEMBER THAT TIMES CHANGE

Time heals all, including the basis for your rejection.[8] It is conceivable that if you wait out an adverse situation, the rejection you have been receiving will turn to acceptance. Larry, an occupational health specialist is a case in point. For years, his company barely tolerated his activities, often hinting that he was a troublemaker rather than a contributor to the company. Gradually, the climate of acceptance shifted.

As health legislation mounted for dealing with problems such as cancer-producing substances in the work place, Larry experienced a surge in power. Instead of the company rejecting most of his suggestions for the prevention of employee poisoning, Larry's ideas were now accepted.

The idea of changing to acceptance over time also applies to some aspects of social life. At one time frail, sensitive males faced rejection by women. By the mid-1970s, these same superficial characteristics became an asset in attracting women. Thus a man who was rejected by women frequently in his early twenties, might have found he was the current desirable stereotype when in his thirties. Similarly, if you felt excluded as a racquetball player in the early 1970s, you are now popular in the early 1980s.

"Remember That Times Change" is a simple application of the problem-solving method. You choose do nothing as one of your alternatives. Similarly, if an executive decides not to go ahead and purchase a new building, that executive has made a decision.

DON'T PUT ALL YOUR EMOTIONAL EGGS IN ONE BASKET

You are hurt most by rejection from the people who are closest to you. Thus, you are likely to hurt more when spurned by your lover or spouse than by casual acquaintances.

You also can be emotionally hurt by rejection on a job, especially if that job is an overwhelming part of your life. The termination will hurt much less when you have some alternatives to explore facing you immediately. Gloria, a former newspaper columnist for the *Dispatch*, expresses this situation aptly.

I made a mistake I won't repeat. The *Dispatch* had become my entire professional life. I worked my way up from the mailroom to having my own column. Some people considered 'Gloria's Corner' the best feature of The *Dispatch*. I thought I saw trouble brewing when we were bought by a large newspaper chain. But I buried my head in the sand, and kept on hacking out my beloved column. Finally the new publisher told me my columns would be terminated. It wasn't professional enough for our new image. He considered my column to be basically small-town gossip.

I felt like a woman whose husband walks out on her after twenty-five years of a good marriage. I have a new job now with another newspaper. But it's strictly a business relationship. I'm also doing a few small things on the side. Never again am I going to invest all my emotional energy in one place. It hurts too much when the relationship sours.

"Don't Put All Your Emotional Eggs in One Basket" is a manifestation of perspective building. Although one job, or one person, may mean a lot to you, you must keep that aspect of your life in proper perspective. That one job, person, hobby, or anything else should not have exclusive claim on your emotional attachment.

NOTES

1. Based on information in Manuel J. Smith, *When I Say No, I Feel Guilty* (New York: The Dial Press, 1975). Bantam edition, 1975, pp. 104–115.

2. *Ibid.*, p. 115–119.

3. *Ibid.*, pp. 120–132.

4. Florence Seaman and Anne Lorimer, *Winning at Work: A Book for Women* (Philadelphia, PA.: Running Press, 1979), pp. 82–84. Running Press is located at South Nineteenth Street, Philadelphia, PA. 19103.

5. *Ibid.*, p. 85.

6. *Ibid.*

7. Andrew J. DuBrin, *Survival in the Office: How to Move Ahead of Hang On* (New York: Van Nostrand Reinhold, 1977), pp. 129–131.

8. Seaman and Lorimer, p. 50.

chapter five
HANDLING SETBACKS
IN COMPETITION

Allow me to express thanks here to my family podiatrist, Dave, not for what he did for my feet, but for what he did for my mind. Several years ago Dave and I were embroiled in a tennis match, played at the club to which we both belonged. At stake was temporary ownership of ninth position on the men's "A" ladder. If I won the match, I would move up from tenth position to ninth position.

Dave and I were familiar with each others' games, having played some twenty-five times previously. The afternoon in question was gusty and chilly. I got off to an early lead in what is termed a pro set. The first player to win eight games would be declared the winner. At one point I was ahead five games to one. Dave closed the gap and the score was soon five to four. As the match moved toward a conclusion, I was ahead seven to four. My concentration waned under the pressure, and Dave tied the score at seven all.

Under the rules imposed by the club, a seven-all match would immediately be thrown into a tie-breaker. The first person to win five points would be declared the winner. Due to one bad bounce, one fine shot, and two errors on Dave's part I was ahead four points to nothing. I could see my name occupying ninth position as we exchanged sides of the court (a required procedure under the rules of a tie-breaker). All I needed to do to win the match was to win one point out of the next five, a pedestrian feat considering that I had already won about half the points in the match. But that last winning point eluded me. Dave won the next five points and the match.

Over a cold drink I said to Dave, "Isn't that incredible, I had you four points to zero in the tiebreaker, and I couldn't win. That's the kind of luck I've been having all season." Dave replied matter-of-factly, "I wouldn't give it a further thought."

Instantly, I realized that Dave was right. If I was going to bounce back from that discouraging defeat, my best strategy was to not give it a further thought. I lost other close matches during that season, yet I succeeded in reducing my choking behavior. The vital strategy of not being concerned about a past loss now has helped me win.

Since the time of Dave's comment, I have been able to concentrate better on the present. The underlying mechanism is that not being preoccupied with the past helps me concentrate better on the present. In the following pages, let's look at additional mental attitudes and strategies for rebounding from setbacks in competitive situations. Although the number of competitive events used as examples will be limited, the same principles apply in many other settings. To illustrate, my podiatrist's advice about a tennis loss can apply also to handling competitive losses in other situations. It might help you in bowling, marathon racing, and poker playing.

REMEMBER THAT AT LEAST HALF
OF ALL CONTESTANTS LOSE

An eleven year old boy engaged his uncle in a one-on-one basketball game on the uncle's driveway. The uncle had a distinct height advantage, 5' 9" to 4' 10". Good-naturedly, the uncle manipulated the situation whereby the nephew was ahead sixteen points to ten (the first player to score twenty points, two points per basket would win). With a smile on his face and a twinkle in his eye, the uncle scored five straight baskets. Final score: uncle 20, nephew 16.

The boy flew into a rage to the point of "accidentally" kicking his uncle. In retaliation the uncle swore to never again play basketball with his nephew because the latter proved to be a sore loser. Not to be outdone, the nephew accused his uncle of committing offensive fouls during the game.

Although the nephew in this anecdote may have been overreacting, his feelings are not atypical. Too many people in our culture exaggerate the importance of winning and overdramatize the negative consequences of losing. With reflection and self-analysis perhaps you can begin to place losing in its proper perspective. At a bare minimum, it is helpful to examine the statistical aspects of losing.

In one-against-one competitive events such as wrestling, boxing, tennis, squash, and ping-pong, half the contestants are declared losers (excluding draws). In tournaments, only one out of a large number (128, 64, 32, 16, 8, or 4) is truly the winner. So from a frequency standpoint, there are far more many losers than winners. You thus should not be too upset over belonging to the majority category. Once you have pondered the statistical aspects of winning and losing, it is helpful to look at some of your feelings on the topic. Many of these feelings, upon close examination, are irrational.

"Remember That At Least Half of All Contestants Lose" is another example of healthy rationalization. You find a logical reason not to be so upset about a competitive loss. You are not denying the fact that you lost nor making the unhealthy rationalization that your opponent cheated, or that you were feeling sick on the day of the competitive event. Losing is inevitable and should be accepted as such.

CHALLENGE YOUR IRRATIONAL THOUGHTS ABOUT LOSING

Losing in competition triggers irrational thoughts, and sometimes irrational behavior, in many people. Irrational behavior refers to such things as throwing a golf club into a stream, breaking a tennis racket on the ground, or publically proclaiming that you are going to quit the sport for life immediately following a loss. Here are some of the irrational thoughts people have about losing that deserve to be challenged:

He's a much better person than I am because he beat me.

I may have a nicer husband, but she's got it over me because she beat me.

From now on, I'm going to feel self-conscious when I see her. She beat me today and has something over me.

If I lose the match this afternoon, what will I tell my family this evening?

People will like me a lot less now that they know I've lost.

It is easy to smirk at other people who entertain such irrational thoughts. But in the heat of competition, many otherwise rational adults and children think in these terms about losing. Underlying all of these irrational thoughts is the premise that losing is bad and winning is good. If you win you are to be held in higher esteem than if you lose. Despite these truths, losing should not lower your self-esteem. If you compete to the best of your ability you should feel some pride in that accomplishment. As the captain of the losing team said to the captain of the winning team, "Congratulations. I thought both teams played very well. You deserve the victory because your team scored two more points than we did."

Another curious fact about losing and winning is that in some forms of competition your approach to the game does more for your reputation than your ability to win. For instance, others may welcome bowling with you because of your sports-like behavior and general ability, not because of how many times you were high scorer for the evening. In public park and club tennis, people develop reputations among other players for the general soundness of their games. Their won and loss record in the park or club is of secondary importance.

"Challenge Your Irrational Thoughts about Losing" relates to self-esteem theory which contends that much of life is a struggle to preserve self-esteem. Some of the irrational thoughts concerning losing come about because you try to protect your self-esteem. If you recognize that this mechanism is working, you might be better able to accept losses gracefully. Losing is also easier to accept when you realize that the importance placed on winning in our society is just a question of values. Somehow we have decided that winning in competition is better than losing.

IT'S ONLY A GAME

During the 1980—81 college basketball season, the DePaul University team had amassed another superb winning streak. One night the team lost to an underdog team, Old Dominion University. The loss deposed DePaul from the number one ranking in two national basketball polls. Ray Meyer, DePaul's beloved coach of over twenty-five years, stated publically, "We lost, but so what? It's only a game."

If a successful coach such as Meyer can think that way about a loss in major college basketball, why can't you think that way about competitive losses when playing for much lesser stakes? The problem is that at the time a loss is incurred, the competitive activity seems to be a major life event. If you could step back and look at that activity in broader perspective, you might be able to realize that "it's only a game."

The turnabout of a bridge player, Harriet, gives us some insight into the value of taking competition less seriously. She recollects in these words:

I've done pretty well in bridge. I began playing bridge while still a college student. A few years later I got serious and took lessons. I studied the bridge column in the newspaper. I played social bridge twice a week and duplicate at least once a week. My problem was that I wasn't doing as well as I would have liked to have done.

It seemed that I choked at my moments of potential greatness. I might be down to choosing the right one of the two last cards in my hand. I remember one incident very vividly. I held the four of hearts and the three of diamonds. It was my lead. If I led the right card, I would have made a grand slam. Somehow in my mind I knew that the three of diamonds was the right play. Yet I panicked. At the last moment I threw down the four of hearts. One of the opponents covered it with the eight of hearts and won the trick. I goofed.

The same kind of thing happened to me time after time. I just couldn't perform as well as the really fine tournament players in our town. Karen, a sixty-five year old friend of mine, gave me some advice that straightened me out. She told me I never laughed or smiled during an entire evening of bridge. She admitted that bridge players are a pretty sombre crew—but not that sombre. She suggested that I smile at least once each evening or afternoon of bridge.

I got the point. I began to see some of the humor in bridge. I smiled occasionally. Soon I wasn't taking the game quite as seriously. It really helped me with my choking. Since I wasn't taking bridge quite as seriously as I did before, I was a little less tense when trying to execute a demanding play.

Eventually I began to realize that the purpose of bridge was to have fun. It's only a recreational activity, not my career.

When you begin to accept the "it's only a game" philosophy, you are in a good position to rebound from loss. Since a competitive activity is usually taken up as a diversion or game, a loss should not be allowed to disrupt your life.

"It's Only A Game" is yet another example of the importance of placing things in proper perspective. The mentally healthy person is able to place competitive activities in proper perspective. Such activities are valuable but they are not worth the price of a stress disorder.

IT TAKES ONLY ONE PUNCH

Despite the wisdom of not taking losing too seriously, many people cannot accept such reasoning. To them, winning is so important that only the prospects of a future win will ease the pain of a present loss. If this characterizes your attitude about the importance of winning, experiment with the *one punch* philosophy. Visualize yourself as the prizefighter who is behind in the fight. Bloodied and bruised but still afoot, you keep thinking to yourself, "Just one good punch and I will win."

The one punch strategy also has relevance outside the ring. Suppose a person is an unpublished novelist. That individual is facing a highly competitive situation since only one out of 300 first novels ever get published. Each rejection hurts, and is often interpreted as a defeat. A one punch attitude can help keep you going. Just one publisher saying yes could lead to one best seller, which could lead to movie rights, and in turn to fame and riches. Obviously, this is rare, but it takes only one punch in the form of the right novel.

The owner of a small employment agency in California used the one punch strategy to rebound from an unfavorable experience. He and his two partners barely survived the business downturn of late 1979 and early 1980. Because many companies curtailed hiring severely in this period, contracts for finding new employees nose-dived. Banner Associates had to borrow a substantial sum of money to stay afloat. One of the partners suggested that they sell the business for whatever price they could. Once sold, the three of them would be free to find salaried jobs.

Bob Banner would not give up so easily. He explained to his partners, "True enough business has been atrocious lately. Nevertheless, many other Los Angeles area firms in the employment field are making a go of it. We need only one good idea to catapult us forward."

Bob and his two partners agreed to put some of their slack time into thinking of a new service that would bring a surge of business to their agency. The new service would represent their one punch that would turn a business setback to a business boom. The three of them then poured over personnel journals and the business section of newspapers to search for the knockout punch of an idea. It became apparent to them that the big new wrinkle in the employment field was outplacement, also known as career continuation.

Within two weeks, Bob and his associates were mailing out flyers to firms in the area explaining their new outplacement division. Its purpose was to help companies find jobs for fired executives. In addition to finding new jobs for these outplaced executives, the firm would provide them career counseling. The program worked. Enough new business came into the firm to compensate for the lack of old business. When contracts for hiring new employees picked up again, Banner Associates still had the thriving outplacement business.

Here is the one punch delivered by Banner Associate brochure:

> Termination is a traumatic situation for both the individual being released and the manager handling the firing. Furthermore, it is a potentially hazardous situation for the firm itself in terms of public image and possible costly liabilities.

> Leading business decision-makers across the country have discovered that by using professionally designed outplacement programs they greatly reduce the trauma of termination for everyone involved. By offering quality career continuation counseling to terminated executives, responsible firms are saving thousands in reduced severance costs. Also, these firms are minimizing potential problems of dealing with job discrimination complaints. Simultaneously they maintain a healthy corporate image for the general public, stockholders, remaining employees and future management recruits.

Approximately eighty percent of executives who participate in out-placement programs are relocated within three to six months. As-toundingly, nearly two-thirds of these executives move to positions with higher salaries or more rewarding job assignments than the positions they left.

How does this outplacement service fit into the general theme of re-bounding from setbacks in competition? The point is that keeping a business profitable during hard times is a highly competitive undertak-ing. Banner Associates was losing out in competition. The recovery punch they delivered was their outplacement service.

"It Takes Only One Punch" fits into a peculiar economic and human law: when the probability of success is low, the payoff is often high. If you keep exploring different alternatives, you might hit upon the one with a low probability of success that has a big payoff. Diamond hunters, movie producers, and lottery players all use the one punch philosophy to cope with setback.

REALIZE THAT LIFE WILL GO ON

Emotionally and intellectually accepting the fact that life will go on despite your setback is useful in recovering from a host of adverse situations. The strategy works in a direct and straightforward manner. Although you are emotionally wrapped up in your loss at the moment, you remind yourself that the loss has no real long term effect on your life. Within an hour or so from the moment of loss, life will go on as usual.

The life will go on strategy is illustrated by the comments of Rich, a young downhill skier. He was interviewed an hour after he had taken a tumble in a race. Rich told us,

What the heck, I sure did wipe out today. It was my second run and you only get two runs. I went down the course in a mediocre time for my first run. I really needed a fast second run. Everything started out just fine as I got off to a good start. No skids, no wasted body motion. It seemed that my time was terrific.

With about five gates to go, I blew it. Somehow the tip on my left ski caught a piece of ice. I tried to flick my ski up quickly. I began to lose control. I tried to lower my body before it was too late but I started to tumble. I rolled over a few times. I wasn't hurt, but I screwed up for the day. I'm officially listed as Did Not Finish.

But no problem. I'm heading back on the bus in a few minutes. The other kids and I will be goofing off on the bus as usual. I'll go out to the movies with my friends tonight. Life will be the same tomorrow. I'll be back skiing on Monday after school. No sweat.

One of my researchers interviewed Cliff, a man who has distinguished himself in tennis tournaments for super-seniors (fifty years and older). Asked how he handled being upset in a tournament by an unranked player, Cliff replied:

I'm usually very down on myself. I fret and I fume. I wonder if I'm finally starting to slip. I ask myself whether I should be still playing the game competitively.

Usually those feelings last until I'm halfway through a warm shower. By the time I'm back in my street clothes, I'm fully recovered. I get back my senses. I realize that by Monday my life will return to normal. I'll be back in the office dealing with the really important problems in my life. I noticed that even if I've won a small tournament, life on Monday is not much different than if I lost in an early round. It's back to the wife and the job no matter what.

Maybe if I made my living as a tennis player, winning or losing would have a bigger impact on my life. Win or lose on the court, my life proceeds on its own merits.

"Realize that Life Will Go On" is not an unhealthy rationalization. It is another example of learning how to keep things in proper perspective.

THERE'S ALWAYS ANOTHER CHANCE TO WIN

Kirk Kerkorian, a one time high roller in the gaming casinos of Las Vegas, became a successful business executive. His view of losses in business was based on his days as a gambler: "Sometimes you lose, but that's the nature of the game. There's always another game and another chance to win."[1] The same attitude is of obvious benefit in placing into proper perspective your losses in competition.

One of the best adjusted men I know is George, a superintendent at a General Motors plant. A man in his fifties, George has coached Little League Baseball for over a decade. My verdict about George's superior adjustment is based on his relationships with his family, subordinates, and Little Leaguers. George has a stable and cohesive family. Both his two adult children and his high schooler rely upon him for emotional support and counsel. He and his wife are a solid team. George is well respected as a professional manager by his supervisors. The youngsters on his Little League team adore playing for "Mr. B." Yet his won and lost record for coaching has not been exceptional.

The clincher for me in reaching a verdict about George's emotional adjustment concerns his attitude toward Little League baseball. George explained to me his philosophy of Little League coaching:

> The bottom line for me is whether or not the boys and gals on the team have some fun. I'm not trying to build a group of someday superstars. Some of the coaches in our league have a warped version of the purpose of Little League. I think you know the guy I'm thinking about in particular. Everytime he steps out on the field, he thinks he's coaching the New York Yankees in the seventh game of the World Series. I think you were there when he threw his clipboard some thirty feet up in the air. One of his ten year olds forgot to step on the plate when she came home. The umpire called her out after the catcher tagged her with the ball.
>
> It's inevitable that some of the kids will take losing very hard. I've had pitchers break into tears when they were shelled by the other team. My job is to get them away from that attitude. I explain to them that it's a long season. If we lose one game we forget about it and try to play a little better in the next game.
>
> If we lose one day, it's not that big a problem. I try to help the kids realize that there will be plenty more chances to try again. If I teach one thing, it's not to take any one game too seriously.

"There's Always Another Chance to Win" can be viewed as a creative application of the problem-solving method. Specifically, you clarify the problem and select a sensible alternative such as trying harder in the next game.

DUST YOURSELF OFF

The beauty of most cliches is that used as originally intended, they have profound meaning. *Dust yourself off and start all over again* is a case in point. This cliche could have been appropriately originated by a rodeo cowboy. After being thrown from a horse onto the ground, the only useful alternative is to literally remove some of the dust from your body and clothing, and try again. Instead of agonizing over your defeat you make a small adjustment and return to competition. Here are several applications of this common sense strategy:

- An adventuresome individual, you take up surfing while on vacation in California or Australia. By the fifth day of your vacation, you are ready to ride a medium-size wave onto the shore. As you get your body positioned, the surfboard flips out from under you. Upon hitting the ocean backwards, you are temporarily blinded by the water in your eyes. Your back smarts from the impact. You are concerned about your vacation partner laughing at you. No matter, brush the water out of your eyes and start all over again.

- You are competing in what seems to be the most important competitive event in your life—the annual company-sponsored golf tournament. You find yourself in a sandtrap on the fourth hole. Concentrating on the ball as carefully as you can, you swing your iron in a swift and graceful motion. Suddenly you are covered with sand, yet the ball has dribbled only about ten feet forward. Your optimum strategy is to brush yourself off and start all over again.

- You are skiing in a minor form of competition. You are trying to impress the person you are skiing with. As you navigate down a difficult hill, you awkwardly lose your balance. Snow works its way into your midriff and your pride is hurt. Instead of cursing or making jokes about yourself, you simply brush some of the excess snow from your clothing (and midriff) and continue on your journey down the hill.

"Dust Yourself Off" is more complicated than it appears on the surface. It relates to the reality principle that you are willing to endure some inconvenience or pain in the present to achieve the pleasure of reaching a longer-term goal.

GET BACK UP ON THE HORSE
THAT THREW YOU

Although this strategy is similar to the dust yourself off strategy, it has a slightly different twist. The rationale underlying *get back up on the horse that threw you* centers on overcoming fear. An accident, near-accident, or other painful experience in competition will usually diminish your desire to compete again. The longer the interim between that uncomfortable situation and the return to the sport, the more inhibited you become. Similarly if you have been involved in an automobile accident, the longer you wait to return to driving, the more fearful you become of driving again. The bouncing-back strategy, then, is to return as soon as possible to the competitive situation which caused the accident.

Speaking in front of a group was one situation Adele, a purchasing agent, dreaded. Since the group would be judging her performance, Adele regarded public speaking as a highly competitive situation. Realizing that her career might be blocked if she could not overcome this fear, Adele enrolled in an effective-speaking class in an adult education program. The day finally arrived for Adele to give her presentation.

Catastrophe of all catastrophes, Adele stood speechless in front of the class. Her mind went blank with respect to all the things she had prepared to say. The instructor recognized her problem as stage fright and gave Adele the sage advice, "If you sit down and relax, your thoughts will return. If you prefer, you can wait until the next class to present your talk."

Adele sat down and immediately analyzed what was happening to her. She reasoned that if she left this class today without speaking, she could never face them again. Adele entertained thoughts of running to the registrar's office and dropping the course. Toward the end of the class session, Adele made her commitment to give the talk. Somehow her fright diminished enough for her to walk to the front of the class. This time her words flowed freely.

Adele's effort to overcome her fear of speaking proved successful. She finished the course as a reasonably adequate speaker. Today she is able to make a presentation as her job sometimes requires. Had Adele not remounted the horse that threw her, she might have developed a permanent inhibition about speaking before a group.[2]

"Get Back Up on the Horse" can be viewed as a form of psychological reconditioning, or desensitization. You learn to overcome fear by placing yourself back in the fearful situation. When used as a form of therapy, you return to the fearful situation in a very gradual manner. If you were involved in an auto accident and now feared driving, your first step might be to simply sit behind the wheel of a car for five minutes. This strategy fights fears by facing them.

ANALYZE YOUR MISTAKES

One of the best ways of bouncing back from setbacks in competition is to analyze what you did wrong that contributed to your loss. In this way you can adjust your strategy or technique to increase your chances of performing better the next time you compete. Before you can do a proper job of analysis, you have to calm down enough to take a somewhat objective look at your own performance. Implicit in this strategy of analyzing your own mistakes is the assumption that winning or improving your performance is something you value. If you can derive the enjoyment you seek from competition without improving your performance or winning, the strategy is not particularly relevant in your case. Here are a few different applications of analyzing your mistakes in order to bounce back from setback:

Sam and his opponent went into the eighteenth hole of a golf match tied at 92. Sam's opponent was the first to finish the hole, with a final score of 97. Sam's score is 95, as the ball now lies about six feet from the eighteenth hole. If Sam sinks the putt, he wins 96 to 97. If he misses the shot the best he can do is tie at 97, forcing the match into a playoff. If Sam needs more than two putts he will lose.

Sam can feel the tightness in his neck muscles as he lines himself up for the putt. Even his wrists are tight as he visually draws a straight line between the ball and the hole. Sam takes a short, three-inch backswing, and moves his putter against the golf ball. It eases to a stop two and one half feet from the cup. Now the score is 97 to 96. Sam still needs to sink the routine two-and-one-half-foot putt to even the match. He lines up the ball and the cup once again, this time feeling even tighter than on the previous shot. Sam does it again. His ball lands three inches in front of the cup. Sam finally sinks the shot but loses the match, 98 to 97. No money or prize is involved, just Sam's ego.

The day after the match Sam makes a candid analysis of what he did wrong.

> I tightened, that's what. I choked because I was just too damn tentative in my putts. I stroked the ball with less power than a pussycat. Next time I'll be more of a tiger. I would have won, or at least thrown the match into a playoff, if I had used normal force on the shot. Next time things will be different. I'll be less tentative under pressure.

Maybe Sam will not succeed, in his next match. Yet his diagnosis of what went wrong is eminently sound. Many people tighten up so much in competition that they turn in a meek performance.

Kate and Reggie are semifinalists in a dance contest. If they can turn in one more win, they will both fulfill a fantasy of winning a trophy. In this contest, the first and second place teams are both recipients of a trophy. Dressed in their favorite competitive attire, Kate and Reggie are a pleasure to watch. As they move into their routines, both sense a little stiffness in their approach. They seem too wrapped up in themselves and not wrapped enough in the music. Kate and Reggie wonder if the judges will detect the stiffness.

Somehow the judges did pick up that barely perceptible variation from the movements of a top dance-pair. Final score by the judges, Donna and Bruce 89, Kate and Reggie, 81. Disappointed by finishing second, but not humiliated, Kate explains what went wrong:

> No sour grapes, but we're really a better team than Donna and Bruce. We can do moves they can't touch. Give them credit though, we made the mistake. Reggie and I just got too aware of ourselves. It's almost as if we were looking at ourselves in the mirror instead of just letting the dancing come naturally. We thought too much of ourselves and not enough about dancing. I could read it in Reggie's face and he could read it in mine. Too bad, but the judges also could see that small touch of stiffness.
>
> The experience was good for us. We'll be less aware of ourselves the next time we enter a contest. Under ordinary circumstances, we're as loose as anybody.

Assistant professor Letty was intent upon working her way up the academic ladder in the sociology field. An important rung on this ladder is to present scholarly papers at national and regional meetings of sociologists. Letty had been doing some intriguing research about how women in business find higher ranking executives to act as their sponsors. She figured that if she could get this paper ready for the April 30 submission deadline, it would be accepted. In Letty's evaluation, if the paper were accepted, and delivered at the meeting, it would get the press coverage it deserved.

Letty did get the abstract of the paper into the mail before midnight, April 30th. Two months later Letty's manuscript was returned with a cryptic rejection note attached. The note read, "Content quite good, but methodology too loose. Resubmit when statistical analysis is reworked." Letty was at first enraged and shocked. How could the American Sociological Association reject such a socially relevant paper?

Letty's post-mortem analysis performed at the gentle request of her department head came up with this penetrating piece of self-criticism:

> Agreed I'm at fault. I have this fabulous piece of research that so far has not been accepted at the national meeting. My work is sound. What went wrong is that I procrastinated too long before analyzing my data. I think I gave myself just a few days, where I should have spent an entire week on the analysis. If I hadn't rushed I wouldn't have done such a spotty job. A careful job might have resulted in my paper being accepted. I'll know better next time.

> My career has received a momentary setback, but that won't stop me from presenting my paper at some other professional meeting. From here on out, no more procrastination when the stakes are big. I learned my lesson.

"Analyze Your Mistakes" is a valid general-purpose coping technique that is really the first step of the problem-solving method. You must clarify the problem before attacking it.

REMEMBER THE VALUE OF LOSING

A closing thought about bouncing back from competitive losses is to recognize that losing has an inner value. It is important, as previously stated in this chapter, to maintain a proper perspective of losing. Losing can help you find out how good you really are. Losing also helps you test your potential. Until you lose at least once, you lack sufficient feedback on the outer limits of your skill. Imagine yourself as a wrestler who has beaten all your opponents. To find out how good a wrestler you really are, it would be necessary to wrestle some tougher opponents. The authors of *Maximum Performance* offer this analysis on the value of an occasional loss:

> The person who has never made a mistake or lost a race has never discovered his limits and has never really joined the human race. Man is not designed to live an error-free existence. Every one of his internal functions—breathing, body temperature, heartbeat—is maintained by a constant search between too-high and too-low limits. In all our behavior we hover between too-much and not-enough, too-far and too-near, too-fast and too-slow. At every moment, we are bumping against our physiological limit settings, locating what's right by finding what's wrong.[3]

"Recognize the Value of Losing" is another valid application of goal theory. After you have set some easy goals for yourself, you raise your level of aspiration until you finally set your sights a little higher than your present capability. The high-level goal helps you measure your potential, much like building up your ability to lift weights by gradually increasing the amount of iron you pump.

NOTES

1. "Kerkorian's Cold Streak," reprinted by permission from *Time, The Weekly Newsmagazine*, July 27, 1970, p. 65. Copyright Time, Inc. 1970.
2. Concept and the anecdote both contributed by Kimberlee McDonald.
3. Laurence E. Morehouse and Leonard Gross, *Maximum Performance* (New York: Simon & Schuster, 1977). Copyright © 1977 by Laurence E. Morehouse Ph.D. Reprinted by permission of Simon & Schuster, a Division of Gulf & Western Corporation.

chapter six
RECOVERING FROM FINANCIAL PROBLEMS

Bouncing back from financial problems requires much more than a practical knowledge of personal finance and money management. You need to buttress your knowledge of facts with attitudes and strategies that will prevent you from again succumbing to financial pressures. For instance, it is valuable to know that, on the average, money market funds pay three times the interest paid by daily savings accounts. It's more important, however, to resist temptation so that you have a surplus of money at the end of the month to invest. Once you have the surplus, you can make some astute financial decisions about where to invest your money to combine high yield and relative security for your capital. Fancy financial footwork can be exercised only after you have acquired the mental resolve not to spend all your earnings. No surplus, no investments.

My position concerning finances is that before you can think seriously about getting rich or breaking even, you have to break loose from energy-draining financial entanglements. If you follow the advice outlined in this chapter, you soon will be able to multiply your capital.

Not everybody has a serious interest in becoming rich. Most of us would settle for getting our financial house in enough order whereby we could escape the emotional turmoil of money problems. A case in point is a man who is now the publisher of a New England newspaper. At an earlier stage in his career, he made a casual statement which might serve as a guiding light for millions of financially troubled people: "I've never felt better in my life. This morning I made my last payment on our refrigerator. I have no debts (he wasn't including his mortgage). I feel like a millionaire, with no more money worries, ever."

CONCENTRATE ON ONE BILL AT A TIME

After speaking to a financial counselor, Heath and Judy were inspired to take a critical look at their financial predicament. After seventeen years of marriage they had acquired an upsetting level of debt. Part of their problem was the debt they had accumulated in the process of acquiring two, two-family houses which they used as income property. According to the plan laid out by the counselor, Heath and Judy needed to scrutinize both their debts and their spending habits.

Heath and Judy's list of debts did not include mortgage payments on their own home, since it has become conventional practice not to consider a mortgage as a debt. If you consider a home mortgage payment a debt, the result would have been even more depressing. (A twenty-five year mortgage, on a median-priced house, with interest included can be close to $100,000 presently). Heath and Judy in an effort to clarify their financial situation compiled this list:

TYPE OF LOAN	BALANCE ON LOAN	APPROXIMATE MONTHLY PAYMENT
Auto	$1850	$185
Home Improvement	975	49
Visa	428	30
Master Charge	859	45
Furnaces for Income Furnaces for Rental Property	1562	65
Tuition	250	60
Orthodontist	750	75
	$6674	$509

In today's economy an indebtedness of $509 per month may not seem outlandish. Nevertheless, in terms of their other living expenses, including the support of three children, $509 per month was creating stress for Heath and Judy. The strategy used by the couple in reducing their debts was to concentrate first on the variable-payment debt with the smallest balance. In other words, concentrate first on the debt that is capable of being eliminated first. Following this strategy, Heath and Judy began their debt-reduction program by first diminishing the Visa debt. Each month they would put as much money as they could spare into their Visa payment even though they had previously paid only $30 monthly for that particular bill. As Judy suggested one day, "Let's throw all our spare change into this cup for the month. Whatever is in the cup at the end of the month goes to attack the Visa balance." And Heath countered with, "Okay, next Saturday night we don't dine out. Instead we'll make a spaghetti dinner and I'll put twenty-five extra dollars toward the Visa account."

Another strategy the couple used was to skimp on payments to Master Charge until Visa was eliminated. The underlying strategy is the same; do whatever you can to eliminate one of your debts. Then go on to eliminating the next loan for which variable payments are possible. In Heath and Judy's case, Master Charge got the ax after Visa. Then came a total thrust against the tuition loan, by making a couple of double payments. By concentrating on the loan with the smallest balance, that loan will soon be liquidated.

A financial expert might rightfully contend that some loans are not economically feasible to discharge more quickly than required. The reason is that their interest rate is lower than the interest you might obtain by investing your extra payments elsewhere (such as money market certificates). While this is true from an economic standpoint, from a mental health standpoint the biggest return on investment is getting out of debt. Within a few months after implementing this plan, Heath and Judy had eliminated $90 from their monthly indebtedness. Owing $419 per month was much less tension-provoking than owing $509.

Within twenty months, Heath and Judy had reduced their monthly payments to a comfortable $95 per month. While on their *Concentrate on one bill at a time campaign*, they were forced to finance a hot-water heater for one of their two-family houses. At last report, the couple is quite optimistic about their financial future. Inflation has helped increase the value of their income property and they are beginning to see a money surplus occasionally. As Judy noted, "Two months ago we actually had a thirty-three dollar balance in our household checking account. It gave me a pleasant tickling sensation inside."

"Concentrate on One Bill at a Time" is more psychologically oriented than apparent on the surface. Its psychological underpinning is that debt creates stress for most people, thus producing tension and anxiety. When you remove a big chunk of that debt, you have eliminated one more stressful aspect in your life.

PAY ON A CASH BASIS

Futurists revel in the fantasy of a cashless society. Some of them contend that electronic transfer of funds, credit cards, bank debit cards (a plastic card that instantly transfers money from your bank account to the account of the merchant) will eliminate the need for cash. Today's high technology may make the cashless society a distinct possibility, but in the meantime don't dismiss the value of cash in helping you recover from sloppy financial habits.

An inescapable conclusion about personal bankruptcy is that no one ever went bankrupt who operated on a strictly cash basis. Cash also refers to money orders and checks drawn against funds you legitimately have on hand. If you do not borrow money, you can never go bankrupt. If you only buy things that you can actually pay for at the moment of purchase, you may suffer some hardships. It is no fun riding the bus or walking until you can save enough money to have a new transmission put in your car. It would be agonizing if you needed dental treatment but had to wait until payday to have a broken tooth repaired. On balance, these are small miseries to incur in comparison to the misery of being mired in debt to the point that it disturbs your concentration and interferes with your sleep.

A lawyer had steered a couple through bankruptcy proceedings. Upon having settled matters, the husband was back to his old problem-inducing tactics of pacifying his wife by borrowing money to purchase goods. To cure his wife's post-bankruptcy despondency he made this offer, "Tell you what honey, we'll borrow some money from my brother and borrow your mother's car and go to the beach with the kids."[1] His wife reacted with rage to his plan for borrowing money. The couple talked it over the following morning with their lawyer who had called them together to sign some papers. The lawyer lost his temper and attacked the couple:

> You two haven't learned a thing. Mrs. Phillips, you are still a whining self-centered woman. Mr. Phillips, you are back on the same old track of pacifying your wife in the name of love and family. Take this vacation if it will do you any good and she can accept it graciously, but I want to tell you something. There are some people who can handle debt and some who cannot handle it. We're both aware that our economic structure is based on the intelligent and responsible assumption and discharge of debt. But Jim, you cannot cope. Go on a cash basis for the rest of your life, like an alcoholic sticking to your ginger ale. Promise yourself![2]

A well-known statistical fact about cash purchases is that people tend to make fewer purchases when they use cash. You are therefore less likely to get into financial hardship if you buy with cash only. A lesser-known psychological fact about cash purchases is that using cash gives you a feeling of power.

Suppose you had been operating under such tight financial conditions for years, that all your consumer purchases were financed with bank credit cards. Because of your high monthly payments, you almost never had enough cash for anything but food, beer, and whiskey. Gradually, by practicing prudent financial management (and using the one bill at a time technique), you finally have some discretionary cash. Imagine how powerful you would feel if you could carry out these kind of activities:

- You walk into a shoe store, find just the kind of boots you want on sale, and say to the clerk "These are a terrific buy. I'll take both pairs. Let me write you a check."
- On the way home from work on a Thursday afternoon (it has been 13 days since the last payday) you pick up concert tickets with cash.
- It's an early spring afternoon so you decide to get started on your yardwork. You realize that your lawnmower needs a complete overhaul. Instead of planning for the overhaul you decide to buy a new mulching mower. You find such a mower at the local hardware store. It's not on sale, but that doesn't bother you because it is just what you want. You make the $285 purchase with cash on hand in one of your drawers.

"Pay On a Cash Basis" relates to both the reality principle and tension management. You postpone the immediate gratification that stems from charging something to achieve the longer term peace of mind that derives from being out of debt. A note of caution is that overcoming the charging habit might prove as difficult as overcoming an addiction to food, gambling, or coffee.

WORK OUT A SETTLEMENT PLAN

People pushed to the point of bankruptcy are sometimes able to avoid the final step by working out some sort of compromise with their creditors. A settlement plan is reached that provides some repayment to the creditors and preserves the pride of the debtor. Gil Brooks, C.L.U. (a designation of advanced competency in life insurance meaning Chartered Life Underwriter) explains how he worked his way out of a complex debt situation by a realistic compromise:

> Approximately ten years ago, I had set up a line of credit with a local bank for premium financing for my insurance clients. I was ultimately responsible for all loans as a guarantor. I thought I knew the principal bank officer quite well. I was to learn differently.
>
> One particular Wednesday I was asked to appear at the bank at 9 A.M. I was ushered into the office of the bank official with whom I had been dealing. Another bank officer accompanied me. Before I knew what was happening, I was subjected to interrogation and beratement by the principal. He ranted and raved about how I had abused the bank. When he tired of this harangue, the "good guy" interrupted and attempted to calm things by saying I had not abused the bank and that I had done my best with the line of credit.
>
> I maintained my outward composure and was ushered out with the understanding that a great deal of work was going to have to be accomplished to satisfy the principal. Several weeks later, I was called by the secondary official. He told me confidentially that the bank was going to recommend that I submit to bankruptcy proceedings. I was told to return to the bank on the following Monday with my attorney.
>
> The amount of the loans outstanding had reached in excess of $135,000. My current assets did not approximate that figure so bankruptcy was my only way out. I went home troubled, the panic

74

inside me having subsided somewhat. I told my wife what the bank was planning to do. We discussed what we had to lose. It was my contention (possibly erroneously) that they could not take our family home which housed ourselves and four children. They couldn't take my car because I needed it for my business.

I was thirty-seven years old at the time. I convinced my wife that we could start all over again since we started with nothing ten years earlier anyway. I formulated a personal plan to fight fire with fire. I intended to go down fighting. One of the first things I was going to do was to insist on a hearing with the state insurance commissioner, and the Banking Commission. I would describe to them in the company of attorneys what I considered to be the unfair position in which I was being placed by the bank.

When I arrived at the bank, I was informed that the previous principal had been fired. I was to be interviewed by a new vice-president. At no time had I been aware that I had been dealing with an incompetent bank official who himself was being pressured by his superiors to get the bank's affairs back into good shape. Many of those affairs had been mismanaged by him personally. My interview was conducted in a completely positive manner by the new official.

Far from wanting to place me in bankruptcy, it was his intention to get my account down to a more manageable size for my circumstances. We were able to accomplish that in the next six months. The bank did not, nor has not, lost a penny on my accounts. I've had a good relationship for approximately six years since meeting the new vice president.

Gil's situation is complex because if his perception is correct, part of his financial problems were complicated by the impulsiveness of a bank official under pressure. Nevertheless the general plan of working out a settlement with creditors is more prevalent than many people believe. To aid financially strapped borrowers many credit companies, banks, and retail stores have stretched out payment schedules on mortages, auto loans and consumer purchases. Sometimes finance charges have been suspended altogether. Many firms consider this type of settlement plan preferable to repossession or foreclosure. Based on their experience, after a borrower declares bankruptcy, the creditor usually recovers very little, if anything.[3]

The punchline is that when pushed against the wall of financial collapse, a settlement can sometimes be worked out which is much better for your self-esteem (and financial well-being) than default.

"Work Out a Settlement Plan" follows along with finding creative alternatives when solving a problem. When embroiled in the emotional aspects of indebtedness, it is important not to neglect exploring all the alternatives facing you.

DEVELOP SPARTAN SPENDING HABITS

An ideal way of returning to or achieving financial health is to increase your income dramatically over the short haul. Unfortunately, few people are in a position to bring about this happy solution. If all your income is derived from salary, increases in your income tend to be gradual. Even if you switch employers, it is rare to attain more than a twenty percent salary increase. Because of sharply accelerated withholding tax schedules, the increase in your take-home pay is often disappointingly small. A strategy more under the control of most people is to work your way back into shape from the expense rather than the income side. Similarly, businesses and non-profit organizations usually cannot increase income as readily as they would like. The firm cannot demand that people purchase their goods and services, nor can the non-profit firm pull strings to immediately obtain a bigger chunk of public funding. Cost cutting and miserly spending habits become the only feasible antidote.

Each individual or family must develop its own spartan spending habits and stick with them until troubled financial times have passed. The combination of reduced spending and salary increase (assuming it matches or surpasses the true effect of inflation on your budget) will help you bounce back from financial woes. Just to stimulate your thinking about what you might be able to do, here are some spartan spending habits developed by others faced with money outgo problems:

- If you pay for your own fuel, wear a hat and gloves inside the house six days a month so you can turn thermostat down to sixty degrees F.
- Switch to cross country instead of downhill skiing to cut down on the cost of equipment, ski-lift tickets, and transportation.
- Jog rather than participating in such expensive sports as golf, tennis, or snowmobiling.
- If you play tennis singles, switch to doubles to reduce expenses for tennis balls, court fees, and shoe wear (you run around less in doubles).

- Eat fruit and carrots or celery for lunch, instead of purchasing lunch or taking costly sandwiches to work.
- Skip purchasing pajamas, night gowns, or housework clothing. Instead sleep and perform household chores in older, worn out clothing.
- Coat your automobile's total exterior, including underside, with rust-retarding paint to delay the rusting process, thus postponing a new car purchase.
- Exchange vital instead of frivolous gifts. Vital gifts include such items as cans of paint, underwear, jeans, kitchen knives, scissors, locks and chains, garment bags, or a tank of gasoline. Gifts like these actually save the recipient money. Since the gift receiver will probably reciprocate, the result is a mutually satisfactory buyer.

"Develop Spartan Spending Habits" is tied in with both the reality principle of delaying gratification and the search for creative alternatives. Use your creativity and look for cost-saving ideas.

FIND VALUE IN POVERTY

While you are developing a game plan to extricate yourself from troubled financial times, your transition will run smoother if you find some value in poverty. One such unanticipated benefit of financial trouble, including poverty, is that a couple or family *sometimes* is drawn closer together. Since they cannot afford to purchase entertainment, they spend more time relating to each other.

Janet works today as a well-paid financial analyst for a large corporation. Her salary combined with child support payments from a former husband allow her and her two children to live comfortably. They take two vacations a year, have a nice house, and save money. But things weren't always so good. Janet explains how in the process of working her way out of poverty, she discovered some of its hidden benefits:

> My financial picture was really grim for a couple of years. Todd, my former husband, helped the best he could with regular child support payments. Yet they only went so far. I needed to finish college in order to qualify for a well-paying job. I scraped together some loans from my parents. I qualified for HEOP (Higher Education Opportunity Program) assistance because I was so poor. We made use of the school lunch program.

I was so embarrassed at first about lots of little things. Sometimes the girls would need five dollars for school supplies and I had to tell them to wait until the first of the month when the next support payment was due. A fellow would ask me for a date and I would have to say no sometimes simply because I couldn't afford a baby sitter.

Soon I realized that total poverty would only last about twenty-four months. I assumed I would get a job right after graduation. So I began to find little ways of enjoying having no money. I met this guy who was kind of broke himself. We made interesting little deals. I would invite him to our little apartment for a dinner date with myself and my girls. All he had to do was bring the meat sauce, spaghetti, and a bottle of cheap chianti. We all had fun and it cost so little.

My girls and I took up fishing. Our gear consisted of a tree branch, a safety pin, and stale bread for bait. We actually caught a few fish which made us laugh. We made gifts for each other out of any scraps we could find such as old pieces of wood or discarded fancy bottles. All our gift and clothing shopping during those two years was confined to garage sales. And we only went on garage sales when a date or relative would drive us.

We survived. I wouldn't want to be poor again. But it wasn't all that bad. Today, I'm still a bit of a tightwad. I can't stand to waste anything. If I'm sent a letter and somehow the post office missed cancelling the stamp, I'll remove that stamp gingerly and use it on one of my letters.

Biographical sketches of famous people sometimes provide insight about how they found beauty in the poverty they encountered on their way to financial success. Robert Redford is an excellent example. The famous actor, producer, and environmentalist recalls that through all those discouraging times in his life when he was broke and unemployed, he was never concerned that it might become a permanent condition. He fondly looks back at these temporary setbacks as having made possible what he is today. In his words:

Poverty never frightened me. It was stimulating; it put an edge on things. It gave me a kind of nervousness which was good. In some sense, I think I'm healthier when things are toughest, and more restless and worried when things are too easy. I always had confidence in my own ability to survive whatever came along. I worry constantly about getting soft and comfortable, but I never worry about suddenly finding myself broke again. I'd survive.[4]

"Find Value in Poverty" might be interpreted as an application of the power of positive thinking. You cope with the present adversity by searching for its positive aspects. Prisoners sometimes utilize this strategy by learning a new skill or trade during their confinement. They might not like being imprisoned, but they salvage something from the situation. You can apply the same strategy to your financial situation.

MODIFY YOUR LIFE STYLE

Earlier in this chapter, developing spartan spending habits was suggested as a way of weathering financial storms. A more sweeping spproach is to modify your life style to match your current discretionary income. For some people on the verge of bankruptcy, this could mean selling their house and moving into a small apartment. The equity received from the sale would be used to clear away debt. The lifestyle shift would be from that of a house dweller to an apartment dweller. A similar lifestyle change would be to move to a lower rent area, and have your older children attend evening, instead of day, college.

Barry, a laid-off middle manager from one of the major automotive firms, was faced with economic hardship. After three months of unemployment, he was able to obtain an engineering position at two thirds of his former salary. His lifestyle change involved several aspects. For one, the family relocated to the Chicago area and rented a house in a middle-income section of town. They were able to rent, but not sell, their Detroit home. His daughter Kathy was told that her parents could no longer send her to private college away from home. Her solution was to live with them, take a clerical job, and attend evening college. In addition, Barry and his wife sold their second car. Asked about how he liked his change of life style, Barry commented,

> Who said anything about liking it? I don't like it, but I have no choice. I'll be back on top someday, then I'll worry about living the way we used to. In the meantime, the whole family is eating. My wife is looking for a job. My daughter is progressing in her education. And I'm able to sleep at night. I know guys laid off from my plant who have it much worse.

Divorce is a major contributor to financial setback. Often both the man and woman are forced to adopt a life style that matches their new economic circumstances. If the man or woman financially strapped in this manner does not make a lifestyle change, the result can be economic calamity. The estranged wife of a dentist tried living after her divorce in the same style she did before her divorce settlement was agreed upon. The result was financial chaos. She describes what happened:

> Before we reached a final settlement, the children and I lived as we did when the family was together. I worked about three days per week in the cosmetic section of a large department store. That helped a little, but it didn't make a bit of difference in our budget. While Marty, my ex-husband, was still paying all the bills, we continued along with the golf club and Florida vacations in the spring and winter. Our housekeeper continued to work for us one day a week. Marty's standard of living was about the same except that he now lived in an apartment. I continued to have my hair done twice a week and a manicure once a week.

> Within two months after the final settlement, I realized I was committing slow financial suicide. My expenses were outpacing my alimony and child support by $600 per month. We had to change, and did so by ending the vacations, private schooling for the kids, and my trips to the hairdresser. Marty no longer pays for everything. He just sends us what he agreed to. Someday I'll get a big job or marry another wealthy man. Then we'll live like we used to. In the meantime, I'm leading a different life.

"Modify Your Life Style" is a combination of choosing among the available alternatives and sorting out your priorities. The latter is sometimes referred to as value clarification. Faced with the financial pressures brought about by divorce, the woman in the above case history came to realize that some of her former necessities were actually luxuries.

TRY BANKRUPTCY
AS A LAST RESORT

About 250,000 Americans will publicly admit this year that they are so far in debt they can no longer pay their bills. They have been advised by their friends, attorneys, or both to file for bankruptcy. Under the more honorable form of bankruptcy, Chapter 13 of the Federal Bankruptcy Act, the person does pay some debts to the best of his or her ability. The petitioner (the person going bankrupt) files a list of creditors and an action plan to repay them with a Federal Court clerk. A small filing fee is paid. Creditors then file their claims and are permitted to foreclose on certain assets such as television sets, antiques, or video equipment. Some property is exempt from seizure depending upon the particular state. Most states allow the bankrupt individual to keep some equity in a home, automobiles, tools of the trade, home furnishings, clothing, a life insurance policy, and a modest savings account.

Some people believe that it is easy to obtain credit once bankrupt because you are debt free and unable to file for a petition for another six years. Such is not always the case. Many would-be creditors look askance at people who have declared bankruptcy. Future prospective employers often perceive you as inept for being a poor money manager.

On the positive side, bankruptcy works a bit like a tranquilizer. It calms you down enough to begin the rebuilding process. It is a last resort, but at least it is preferable to being constantly hounded by creditors. A sixty-year old self-employed engineer and building contractor explains how bankruptcy helped place him on the road to recovery:

> I was born and raised in Holland. I'm a nautical engineer by trade. I worked for the Holland-American Shipping Lines until after World War II. Following the war, I moved to America permanently. I worked for other people for a few years, and then I decided to try contracting myself. My business started slowly in New Jersey and gradually grew bigger. More men started to work for me.

> We kept needing new tools to work faster and do more jobs, but we also needed the money to buy them. It was a vicious cycle. My company was in over its head. With my debts far behond my assets, I had to file for bankruptcy. It was a terrible time in my life. The children were small. My wife had to get a job to support us and help pay the mortgage. I thought we would lose the house.

> It wasn't entirely my fault because people owed me money and my collections were very poor. I felt very inadequate and it took a while to straighten things out. I finally started contracting on my own again. Making contacts was hard for a couple of years until my reputation was restored. But now I am back in business. I have twenty fulltime employees and many parttime employees. My business is doing very well.

> Just before filing for bankruptcy was the worst time. I couldn't see

from one day to the next. Everything closed in on me. When bankruptcy finally was decided, it was a tremendous weight off my shoulders. I could at least see some light at the end of the tunnel.

I learned some lessons from going bankrupt. The most important lesson was how to control money coming in and going out. I paid more attention to keeping the books straight. I never forgot those feelings of being without money. It also made me much stronger as a person and a businessman. I learned to believe in myself.[5]

"Try Bankruptcy as a Last Resort" is based on self-esteem theory. To avoid lowering your self-esteem, try all other alternatives before you declare bankruptcy.

GIVE YOURSELF A YEARLY
FINANCIAL CHECKUP

Assume, like most of the people mentioned in this chapter, you have either experienced financial troubles in the past or hope to improve upon your present financial status. An infrequently practiced, but potentially uplifting strategy, is to chart your yearly financial status. If you see any progress, you can rejoice. Progress, in this sense, means that the discrepancy between your assets and liabilities is increasing in a positive direction. In short, your net worth is increasing.

Almost all firms, both profit and non-profit, prepare an annual report. It helps the public and insiders know how they are doing. The annual report recommended here is an abbreviated version for individuals. You include in the report only liquid assets—those you could convert to cash with ease if you so desired. Although the equity in your house is a liquid asset only under favorable circumstances, it's worth including in your annual report. Without house equity included in their balance sheet, most homeowners would have meager liquid assets. Here are two personal annual reports prepared by the same person who was in financial trouble when the first report was prepared. Notice the progress this individual has made in the four year period. In 1977, his liquid assets, aside from his home equity and car resale value, totaled $934. Including house and car, his assets were $17,534. Thanks in part to both self-discipline and inflation, his assets jumped to $28,595 four years later. Without the house equity and car resale value (the car had become a clunker with over 85,000 miles on the odometer) his liquid assets were $3,795.

ASSETS	DECEMBER 31, 1977	DECEMBER 31, 1981
House equity (based on estimated market value)	$14,000	$24,000
Cash in checking account	41	292
Cash on hand	25	215
Savings accounts	18	692
Mutual fund	—	596
Car resale value	2,600	800
Silver, gold jewelry resale value	850	2,000
	$17,534	$28,595

LIABILITIES		
Auto payments	$ 2,500	—
Visa card	1,215	350
Master Charge	1,150	400
American Express	850	50
Sears	450	28
Home improvement loan	2,975	—
Loan from uncle	895	—
Property tax due	850	150
School tax due	450	200
Plumber	275	—
	$11,610	$ 1,178

The liability picture is even more impressive. In 1977, the man had outstanding debts of $11,610. Four years later, his debts had shrunk to $1,178. His liability position had improved a whopping $10,432. Over the same period his asset picture had improved $11,061. Adding both improvements together we can give the individual a financial improvement score of $21,493 for the four-year period.

The yearly financial checkup is thus a potent measure of how well you have rebounded from financial trouble. It also could be used to track the progress of any person who enjoys personal financial planning. A person who practices some of the strategies described in the previous pages at least has the chance of someday gloating over a five-figure improvement score. Even a three-figure improvement score is likely to reduce some of the inner turmoil associated with financial problems.

"Give Yourself a Yearly Financial Checkup" fits the concept of motivating yourself by receiving feedback on your performance. Your yearly financial statement is a valid measure of your financial progress. If you have made progress, it will serve as a reward to keep going along the same path. If the feedback is negative, it could serve as a signal to change your behavior.

NOTES

1. June Mellies Reno, "What It's Like to Go Bankrupt," *McCall's*, March 1975, p. 82.
2. *Ibid.*
3. "Bankruptcy—No Longer a Dirty Word," *U.S. News & World Report*, April 7, 1975, p. 52.
4. Ivor Davis, "Not an Ordinary Person," *Success*, December 1980, p. 46.
5. Case researched by Richard Romano.

chapter seven
RECOVERING FROM A LOST RELATIONSHIP

When you're emotionally and romantically involved with another person, the loss of that relationship usually has a big impact. Even if you can't wait to get rid of your partner, the fact that you cared at one time about that person leads to some hurt. Lost relationships include being dumped, divorced or separated, or widowed. The big reason we need strategies for dealing with lost relationships is that so many upsetting feelings surface in conjunction with the loss. A newly unattached person might feel lonely, guilty, angry, or frightened. Your role in the disengagement will usually dictate which emotion surfaces. For instance, if you dumped your partner, you will probably experience guilt. If you were the person dumped, you would probably experience anger. If you survive a spouse, you might feel guilty about not having been nice enough to your partner during your years together.

As in every other chapter in this book, you should choose from among the strategies those that seem to fit your personality and circumstances. A note of caution that would also apply to most of the advice dispensed in this book: If these strategies do not work for you, your best alternative would be to discuss your problem with a mental health professional, pastoral counselor, or family physician.

BE THANKFUL FOR THE GOOD
IN THE RELATIONSHIP

An excellent starting point in bouncing back from a broken relationship is to take stock of what went right when the two of you were together. Upon splitting, it is natural to overreact and forget that the relationship at one time satisfied some of your needs and interests. Looking for the good that took place in the relationship helps place things in proper perspective. Among the improper perspectives usually voiced at the time of separation, divorce, or splitting, is that the relationship was a waste of time. A person who says angrily, "I gave you the best years of my life," is usually forgetting that he or she received something in return. Mario was so disturbed about his wife asking for a divorce, that he joined an encounter group so he could talk about his feelings. During the second session the group leader confronted Mario with the fact that he had nothing positive to say about his wife. With some additional encouragement from the group, Mario finally put it this way:

> You got me. I've been pigheaded. Yvonne did a lot for me. I'm hurting now, but in the early days of our relationship Yvonne did a lot for my ego. I was an average guy. All of a sudden I met Yvonne, a beautiful woman who actually listened to me. She made me feel like somebody important. I know I'll always love her even though she left me. We have a great little son together. That alone made the relationship worthwhile.

The expression of these feelings did Mario a lot of good. Soon he began to overcome his bitter attitudes toward his lost relationship. It cleared the way for him to begin relating in a realistic way to the women he met. Instead of being overly guarded about getting to know somebody new, he acted more like his former self. He quickly discovered that having recently lost a relationship was neither unusual nor disgraceful.

"Be Thankful for the Good in the Relationship" is an example of the therapeutic value of maintaining perspective. When you take stock of the fact that at one time your relationship brought you pleasure instead of sorrow, your chances of recovery are above average. If you focus on the negative aspects only, you will decrease your chances of bouncing back.

RELEASE SOME OF YOUR ANGER

Mario, the man used as example in the study just described, achieved good results by expressing his positive feelings about his lost relationship. It also can be helpful to vent your anger over the split-up. Strangely enough, some widows and widowers have pent-up anger about their departed spouse. They feel angry about being left alone in the world. Whatever the reason for the anger, there is some value in dealing with it openly.

Psychotherapist Mary Sojourner suggests that a good time to express anger over a lost relationship is once self-confidence begins to come back, nurtured by the support of friends and family. Often the lingering anger is turned inward, creating depression. Sojourner states that, as a therapist, her biggest job is teaching people to be angry. She encourages people to yell about their problem, to pound pillows, and hurl tennis balls against the wall. She contends that the physical expression of anger usually helps break up the log-jam of inner feelings.[1]

For some people, expressing anger works best when it is shared with the person who left you. In other words, tell your former partner in direct terms what you think of him or her. This advice hardly will seem to be something new for the thousands of couples who hurl insults and physical objects at each other prior to splitting. One man received a surprise result when he ventured his true feelings about being dumped by his girlfriend to her. A product of assertiveness training, she replied "Bill, thanks so much for sharing your anger with me."

"Release Some of Your Anger" is a straightforward application of catharsis—reducing your tension by releasing some of your true feelings.

GET YOURSELF DECENT ACCOMMODATIONS

One of the most humiliating and depressing aspects of becoming single again is being forced to move into substandard living quarters. In the traditional arrangement, the male agrees to find an apartment while the wife and child or children remain in the same apartment or house. A close second to this arrangement is for both partners to look for less expensive dwelling. If you must relocate, you should do your best to establish living quarters attractive enough for entertaining while being financially sound. Without a decent place to live, recovering from a split is all the more difficult.

Ted, a high school teacher, broke up with his wife. She continued to live with their two children in a modest but comfortable house. Strapped for cash, Ted moved in with two other male faculty members from the same school who were in the process of divorcing. After two months of this arrangement, Ted expressed his anguish in these terms:

> I've got to get out of that pig sty. My roommates are acting like college kids in a fraternity house. They throw beer cans and orange peels on the floor. I've seen cleaner lavatories in bus stations. The last straw was when I took a date back to the house for a drink. We came in the living room to find one of the guys having sex with his date on the couch. I'm ashamed to have my children visit me at my new place.

Despite strapped financial circumstances, there are alternatives to the option Ted chose. If he chose to share living quarters with other divorced males, he should have been more selective. Few adult males are as sloppy as those described by Ted. For most divorced men and women, the new accommodation of choice is your own place. It is probably best for your mental health to give top financial priority to a pleasant living arrangement. Cost-saving measures are best applied to other areas of living such as clothing, food, entertainment, and vacations.

Recently separated executives sometimes ease their way into single life by moving into a hotel or club. Such a maneuver, however, tends to slow down rather than hasten the adjustment process. Coming home at night to a hotel or club room can be devastating if a person has lived for years in a luxury apartment or house.

A high cost of living area will often make it seem almost impossible for separated people to afford comfortable living quarters. Suppose, for example, the newly separated husband is forced to look for an attractive apartment in New York, Toronto, or San Francisco. Such costs have to be factored in to the financial side of separation agreements. As two-paycheck families continue to proliferate, fewer recently separated individuals will be forced to live in accommodations so substandard that these living quarters prevent a satisfctory adjustment to single life.

"Get Yourself Decent Accommodations" centers on protecting your self-esteem. It will be difficult to cope with a broken relationship if your self-esteem, and therefore self-respect, is shattered through living in accommodations you despise.

FIND NEW OUTLETS FOR SPARE TIME

One possible fringe benefit derived from terminating a close relationship is that you often have more spare time. Instead of obligations such as spending Saturday nights and Sunday afternoons with your partner, you are suddenly able to spend that time as you see fit. In the past, you might have used an occasional Saturday night or Sunday afternoon for your own pleasure, but mild pangs of guilt might have been the price. If an individual invests into new outlets some of the time formerly spent with the estranged partner, the result can sometimes be uplifting.

Clinical psychologist Muriel Oberleder illustrates this principle with the case of a fifty-year-old executive who always wanted to be an amateur actor but never had the time. Subsequent to his divorce, he joined a local theatre group. After two or three plays, the executive found himself involved with a new group of friends, and over the trauma of his divorce.[2]

An intelligent young man, Ron, provides an account of how he found new outlets for his spare time to help him deal with the trauma of separation. In his words,

> An emotional crisis which sticks in my mind is really quite personal. It involves a girl with whom I formed a rather strong relationship. It began as a platonic work relationship but eventually became more complicated. We ended up living together for some two and one-half years. During that time, I worked fulltime as a restaurant manager while she was attending the state university.
>
> As graduation time came nearer, I realized I would be having to make some important decisions about my and our future. I had no intention of tying her down and destroying her career plans, yet sometimes I think she had expected me to. The crisis began when

it came time to break up and move on. I had the option of going with her, which would have ultimately led to marriage. But I was so unsure of what I wanted out of life that I could not make any decision other than going back to life as I knew it before I met her. This meant returning to my parents, which was an uncomfortable situation. The hardest part, however, was saying goodbye to a person whom I shared everything with for over two years. It was almost like a divorce.

I knew that I had to rebuild my life around myself rather than around two people. This meant I would have to forget everything about her and concentrate on other things. It certainly was not easy because I was emotionally shot. Other than missing her, I also realized that my life was regressing while she was moving ahead. My emotional state also hurt my job performance.

The major method I used to cope with the situation was to occupy myself with something else. I enrolled in school, which was something that I had always wanted to do, but just never got around to it. I figured it also would help me to meet other people and at the same time, would help me formulate career objectives. The methods I used to deal with my problem have helped a great deal. I must point out that they have not been one-hundred percent effective, because every now and then I still think about her.[3]

Ron's story is a good example of finding constructive outlets for your energy to help you deal with the post-separation blues. It also illustrates that activities cannot be a complete substitute for a satisfying relationship with another person.

"Find New Outlets for Spare Time" is a healthy form of psychological compensation or substitution. Some of the energy you were investing in your past relationship is now invested in spare time activities. Ironically, it is these same spare time activities that often lead to new relationships.

GET AMPLE REST AND RELAXATION

A broken relationship brings stress. Rest and relaxation are needed to help overcome the emotional pain associated with the departure of a partner. A manual for surviving the loss (not only through death) of a loved one offers these easy-to-apply suggestions.

- Rest.
- Get additional sleep.
- Obtain help with arduous tasks.
- Arrange your life so that you receive ample rest. Schedule rest into some part of your day. Make plans to go to bed earlier and sleep a bit later than usual.
- Proceed about your life gently. Avoid unnecessary rushing around. You need to conserve energy because your body needs to recover from stress.
- Try Transcendental Meditation (TM) because it provides a beneficial state of rest.
- Rest your emotions. Avoid heavy emotional commitments for awhile.
- Remember that rest is the guardian of health.[4]

"Get Ample Rest and Relaxation" is a self-evident form of stress management. Unless you take care of yourself physically and mentally, it will be difficult to bounce back from the lost relationship.

PAMPER YOURSELF

An ageless recommendation for recovering from a broken relationship is to pamper yourself. *Pampering* involves essentially finding little ways of doing nice things for yourself. It could take the form of buying yourself a new outfit, getting a manicure, a massage, taking a weekend vacation, eating a pizza at midnight, sleeping until noon, or having your car repainted. The form of pampering you choose will depend upon your income and your life status. A recently separated mother with custody of a pair of three-year old twins would have a difficult time sleeping late (unless the twins sleep at their father's home).

Fifty-five-year old Harry, a stockbroker, set out to pamper himself after splitting with his wife of twenty-six years. He reports how he received more pampering than he anticipated:

> It was really tough splitting after all those years. The kids were grown and out on their own. My life with Sylvia had become too mechanical for the both of us. It was like a business partnership where the two partners don't communicate. So we tried a trial separation.

I was feeling low, so I figured I would give myself a treat. I decided to go to that famous bathhouse for executives on the east side. Several of my friends went there from time to time and said they were quite pleased with the result. I always wondered what it would be like to be massaged by an expert.

I was pleasantly shocked to find out a little more about the place. A gorgeous young woman was my masseuse. After the hot bath came the gentle massage while I lay down on a table, naked. It cost $45 for a half hour. She then informed me that tipping was allowed. She started to finger the area around my groin as she emphasized the word tipping.

I knew the place wasn't a brothel, so I imagined she couldn't be suggesting too much. I did ask her how much a tip she would need to massage me to a climax. She said "$35 dollars in advance." It proved to be the most relaxing $35 I've spent in years. I guess you could call it a cheap thrill, but it's a nice little treat for myself that I plan to purchase again.

"Pamper Yourself" can be interpreted as a way of taking care of some of your lower order needs. Things like feeding yourself well, taking warm baths, and participating in recreational sex won't do much for self-fulfillment, but at least you will feel better.

USE SUPPORT GROUPS

A well-researched antidote to coping with a broken relationship is to rely upon support groups specifically designed to help recently unattached people. Parents Without Partners is the best known of these groups for separated or divorced parents. Other such organizations are found in most communities. They are sponsored by community centers, churches, and temples. Neutral Ground is the name of one such group to help adults recover from post-separation trauma. You can also receive emotional support from groups with names like The Singletons, or The Phoenix Singles Club. Check the telephone directory and newspaper for clubs, associations or groups.

Peggy, a forty-five your old widow, tells a story that points to both a key advantage and disadvantage of such groups:

Right after John died, I was distraught. We had a wonderful relationship. I realized I couldn't wallow in my own misery forever. It wasn't fair to myself or the children. A friend of mine dragged me to a Parents Without Partners Meeting. Most of the members were divorced or widowed women about my age. They were all so helpful. They seemed genuinely concerned about helping me adjust to becoming a single parent.

They taught me to smile again and look at the positive things in life. I felt much less strange and alone. But after awhile I began to realize I didn't need PWP that much anymore. I felt I could make it myself out in the world. Slowly it became depressing to talk so much about being a single parent or finding another man.

I hope I'm not being selfish. But I took the best from the group and then left on good terms. I would still recommend PWP to any woman trying to adjust to being a single parent. It might be good for some women to stick with them for years. But not for me. I prefer to fend for myself with just the help of one or two friends.

"Use Support Groups" works so well because of the healing powers of love and affection. Almost everybody needs reassurance and comfort in times of trouble. It makes you feel better and helps you rebound.

SEEK EMOTIONAL SUPPORT
FROM INDIVIDUALS

Emotional support can be obtained from others who have suffered a lost relationship. The groups mentioned in the previous section are useful sources for people who will provide you with that type of emotional support. The most potent support comes in the form of other people, including members of your family. These people will reassure you that you are a fine person despite the fact that you are currently alone. Receiving feedback from others that you are still a worthwhile person even though you have been abandoned is a crucial first step on the road to recovery.[5]

Encounter groups, personal growth groups, and counseling groups are a haven for people seeking this kind of stroking. One veteran of these groups, a middle-aged woman, had a knack for giving encouragement to recently separated or divorced women. In one group setting, she delivered this positive stroke to a frightened and unsure newcomer:

> Maggie, your ex-husband obviously had very bad judgment. He'll probably realize how wrong he was very soon. We can all see what a terrific person you are. You have shown us a lot of wonderful qualities. We love you.

To the outsider, it might appear that the veteran personal growth group participant is syrupy. However, at the time, the type of feedback she provides is a potent antidote to a post-separation funk. Family members, too, can provide a valuable psychological service to another family member suffering the pangs of a broken relationship. For confirmation ask the parent whose child says, "I still love you even if Daddy (or Mommy) is angry at you."

"Seek Emotional Support from Individuals" relates to the basic idea about human nature that most people have a need to be nurtured and comforted, and this need is the most active during times of upset in our lives.

GET OUT AND GO PLACES

Getting out and going places is a multi-faceted antidote. Instead of staying preoccupied with your loneliness, you are focusing your mental energy on the outside world. While you are doing new things, you tend to forget about some of your problems. Also, as you proceed about going places and doing things, you increase your chances of making new friends. And new friends are the only true antidote to the loneliness stemming from being unattached.

Where should you go? My recommendations are to go any place where there is some chance of your interacting with other people. Simply going someplace and not responding to other people is not much of a help for loneliness. Passive activities like attending movies, plays, or concerts might be good for pampering yourself but they provide a minimum of interaction with other people. It is far better to go to places where you might be able to smile and laugh with strangers. Here are some suggestions:

- Antique car shows (People love to admire cars with strangers.)
- Zoos (Sometimes you just feel better sharing laughter with children about the antics of chimps or hippos.)
- Sporting events (Strangers enjoy sharing sports trivia and the excitement of the game.)
- Public beaches (You can always start a conversation about the water temperature or purity.)
- Toastmasters (A fabulous way to build your self-confidence through improving your ability to speak in front of others. You are forced to interact with loads of supportive people.)
- State and county fairs (City and country folk alike have loads of fun watching the livestock and carnies. The atmosphere is so informal that you can talk to strangers without being suspect.)
- Company sponsored picnics. (A wonderful way to meet new people and to practice a healthy form of office politics at the same time.)
- Winter carnivals (Snowmobilers are fun loving, heavy drinking people who open up to strangers.)
- Night classes in self-development or hobby topics (Ideal for feeling better about yourself and growing as a person. The underlying antidote to loneliness here is that you share experiences with other adults.)

"Get Out and Go Places" can be a useful antidote to the problems of a lost relationship because it satisfies the basic human need for affiliation and affection. As you interact with others, even on a superficial level, you begin to satisfy these needs, at least partially.

INVITE NEW PEOPLE INTO YOUR LIFE

As a logical follow-up to getting out and meeting people, try to form relationships with some of the people you meet. The people you invite into your life do not have to necessarily become objects of romance. Friends of any type can help compensate for some of the loneliness associated with losing a relationship. One major strategy to allow another person to enter your life is to share interests, rather than talking about your own problems.

If you're asking questions of another person, make sure most of the questions cannot be answered with one- or two-word responses. Here are several well-established conversation openers:

- "Please tell me about your job."
- "What has been your experience with Toastmasters?"
- "Tell me how you have been able to keep your 1967 Buick in such fine shape.
- "What do you think I should do about a father who is too busy to see his children?"

"Invite New People Into Your Life" works because you must open up to and share with people. However, you are likely to get more need satisfaction from the friends you make this way than from casual interactions.

HELP OUT SOMEBODY
LESS FORTUNATE
THAN YOURSELF

Feeling down, lonely, and sorry for yourself? A doubly useful antidote is to find somebody less fortunate than you to help. The antidote is doubly useful because you're helping both yourself and another individual feel better. A sixty-year-old widower explains his experience along these lines:

> God took Emma away from me last spring. It takes a lot to overcome the shock of losing your companion of thirty-six years. I realize I wasn't wiped out. I still have two grown children and four grandchildren. They live in another state, but I still get to see them on occasion. My kids were very helpful during my bereavement.
>
> Soon I realized that I couldn't rely on my own children or grandchildren. I needed to do something on a more regular basis. An advertisement on television was shown which talked about being a Big Brother, that is, somebody who is a companion to one or two young boys who don't have a father or an older brother. I thought I might be too old to qualify, but the idea sounded interesting. I had plenty of spare time with Emma gone.

I phoned the agency that was running the program. The woman in charge told me that I was young enough to be a big brother. I made an appointment with the woman. After filling out the necessary paperwork, I was told that they would be calling me within a few days. They followed through on their promises.

I'm the Big Brother to two poor little guys who have no father and a part-time mother. I love the little rascals. I've been buying them gifts and taking them places. The three of us went to a baseball game the other night. I've even given them some surplus furniture for their living places.

Mind you, I have not forgot Emma. I still think of her, and I know she would be proud of me. I've got a new cause in life and it's doing my mind a world of good.

"Help Out Somebody Less Fortunate Than Yourself" is yet another way of gaining perspective on the gravity of your problems. In addition, most people will find satisfaction in giving direct comfort to others. It can be a direct expression of the need for nurturance.

START DATING FOR FUN

Given a choice, most people who experience a broken relationship will soon start dating again. For some people, soon is the same week as the termination date of the relationship. For other people, soon might be one year after a divorce or the death of a spouse. Whatever your starting point for dating again, it is useful to ponder the consistent advice of experts. Most experts feel that dating should commence merely for recreation, thus avoiding emotional entanglements before you are emotionally prepared to take on another serious relationship. Once your emotions have settled down, serious dating seems to be fine.

A basic reason for avoiding early emotional entanglements is that your vision might be blurred about the new relationship. A woman who was married to a miser might overreact by falling in love with the first big spender whom she dates. Her basis for love might be an overreaction to a major negative characteristic of her former spouse (miserliness). Aside from being a big spender, the new lover might not really have the deeper characteristics the woman requires.

Lillian is an example of how getting emotionally entangled can hurt someone. Her story included these elements:

> I was really taken for a ride by Danny, a handsome young guy. After Lou, my former husband, and I split, I decided that I would once again enjoy sex. Lou might have been enthusiastic about sex in general, but not with me. So I figured, if I started dating again, it would be with a man who found me sexually attractive.
>
> Danny worked in a men's clothing store and looked the part. He was good looking, well-dressed, and smooth. Ironically, I met him shopping for the last gift I bought Lou. Right after Lou and I split, I went shopping in the same store. I guess I was hoping to meet Danny again. I struck up a conversation about how much my ex-husband liked the silk ties.
>
> We met for a drink that evening. Before long, we became lovers. Within three weeks, I invited Danny in to live with me and my daughter. He was an enthusiastic lover. Other than that, Danny was kind of a leech. He borrowed things from me like luggage and a portable television. He told me he needed the television for his ailing sister and that he would have it back soon.
>
> When Danny had borrowed a total of $1800 from me, I thought there was something phony about our relationship. I knew Danny wasn't able to afford all the things he wanted because of his limited salary at the store. However, I didn't enjoy being taken for a ride.
>
> One day after work I arrived home to find Danny's closet empty. He left a note on my dresser saying that he was leaving town but that he would always remember me as a special friend. I haven't heard from Danny since.
>
> What bothered me as much as being made a fool of was all the explaining I had to do for friends. I tried to avoid my friends after I heard the questions they asked about my handsome friend. I think, though, I can profit from this experience. I became infatuated with Danny because of his looks and his sex appeal. I was too blind to see that he was just out for fun and a few bucks.
>
> It's been humiliating, but I think I've learned my lesson. I'll be into casual dating *only*, for a while.

"Start Dating For Fun" can be an effective strategy because it prevents you from developing inhibitions about relating to new people of the opposite sex. It is also related to the concept of emotional insulation. You are going through the motions of dating, but you are at the same time protecting yourself from getting emotionally involved before you are ready.

GIVE EXPRESSION TO YOUR INNER SELF

A lost relationship sometimes leads to the positive byproduct of feeling free to be yourself again. In the process, as you express your inner self, you undergo an exhilarating experience. In many relationships, one individual suppresses the other. For instance, one woman might be basically fun-loving, playful, and adventuresome. But in her interactions with her spouse she is subdued, possibly because she feels uncomfortable in his presence or because he gives no encouragement to these inner qualities. Perhaps she does not even realize what is happening to her. Finally the couple splits, and her inner self emerges. In the presence of her friends (and new lover) she again becomes funloving, playful, and adventuresome.

An experienced psychotherapist explains how the loss of a relationship can contribute to a person's growth and development:

> For most people, being dumped—as painful as it is, as crazy as it sounds to say this—is one of the best ways for people to come to terms with themselves. I can't think of one instance where over the long haul, one or two years later, the people I've known who have been dumped—and have gotten some help with it—haven't been better off for it.[6]

The *better off* the therapist refers to is the freedom to express parts of your inner self that have been suppressed or subdued for years. The moral of this in relation to overcoming adversity is that by allowing your hidden strengths to emerge, you compensate to a large extent for the sorrows of losing a relationship. Vera explains how this principle worked for her:

> If you want to know the good side of my divorce, please take one of my business cards. Believe it or not, that's me, Vera Alstead, freelance photographer. My former husband used to ridicule me when I told him that I wanted to do some commercial photography. He told me there were five thousand people out on the streets trying to

take pictures for a few bucks. I believed him when he said nobody would take me seriously.

When we finally split over other issues, I stepped up my photo activity to get my mind off the agony of separation. Just by casually mentioning to friends that I was willing to photograph their pets and children for pay, I got a few small assignments. One thing led to the next. I expanded my closet-and-sink operation into a full-fledged darkroom. I even sold a few photos to a pet magazine and won a local contest. Now I'm making a living with my photography. I love every moment of it. If my husband and I hadn't split, I never would have developed my talent to the point that I became a real photographer.

"Give Expression to Your Inner Self" is a method of working toward self-fulfillment. As you begin to feel better about yourself, and proud of what you are doing, some of the hurt from the broken relationship will dissipate.

GIVE YOURSELF TIME TO HEAL

A team of people who have dealt with the problem believe that surviving a broken relationship takes time.[7] Following the suggestions in this chapter may help you, but instant cures are not highly probable. A valid generalization is that the greater the hurt, the more time it will take to recover from the broken relationship. Correspondingly, if you left somebody you had grown to dislike, your recovery time will probably be short. Your biggest problem might be in trying to resolve some of your guilt over having split from your partner.

How can the *healing takes time* generalization help you bounce back from a relationship that dissipated? Simple recognition and acceptance of this fact would be helpful in curbing your impatience to disentangle yourself emotionally from your former spouse, or lover. One of the reasons people are cautioned not to date seriously for a while is that they may not be emotionally ready for a new relationship. This lack of readiness may interfere with forming a mutually satisfying new relationship. Such is the case of Bud, a man who aborted several new relationships because he had still not recovered from the blow of being dumped by his former wife. A woman who told Bud she couldn't take competing with his former wife any longer, describes Bud's behavior:

> Bud's a great guy. Well educated, decent looking, and he loves to do things. But he's got to get his head on straight before most women would tolerate him. He's a source of embarrassment, especially when you're out with other people. A typical scenario would run this way: We'd be seated in a restaurant and the conversation would turn to something like housing. Bud would say things like "We had this alcove built," or "We went to Puerto Rico one winter."

> Worse from my standpoint was how he would go on talking about his former wife Janine. He went on at length about how great an artist Janine was or how good Janine was at making omelettes. I finally told Bud to get in touch with me again when he got over Janine. Why go in competition with some ghost from the past?

"Give Yourself Time To Heal" is a way to soften the hurt. This strategy will keep you from getting involved in a relationship which you are emotionally unable to handle.

ANTICIPATE A POSITIVE OUTCOME

All those good things you've heard about the power of positive thinking and raising your expectations apply equally well to recovering from a lost relationship.[8] If you emotionally accept the proposition that losing relationships is an uncomfortable, but almost inevitable, aspect of life, you will have taken the first step toward recovery. There is nothing unworthy, unhealthy, or maladaptive about you because your relationship didn't make it to the finish line. Similar to most people, you will have to start anew.

While you are on the path toward rebuilding your social life, it is crucial to believe that things will get better, that all the emotional energy you have invested into splitting and healing will pay dividends. Self-fulfilling prophesies work to some extent in social relationships. If you believe that you will make a satisfactory recovery from a lost relationship, the chances increase that you will. The underlying dynamic seems to be that because you believe in your recouparative powers, you ap-

proach new social situations with a confidence that sends out perceptible vibrations to others. You believe in you, so the person you are trying
to cultivate believes in you.

Anticipate a positive outcome and you have taken an important
step in making that happy state of affairs come true.

"Anticipate a Positive Outcome" might be labeled the Pygmalion
Effect in bouncing back. As you raise your levels of self-
expectation, you rise to meet these levels. The Pygmalion Effect
has been known to work in improving the grades of students and
the performance of employees. It also should help you rebound
from a lost relationship.

NOTES

1. Sue Dawson, "Getting Dumped," *Times-Union*, Rochester, N.Y., August 23,
   1980, p. 5.
2. Quoted in "Personal Business," *Business Week*, February 9, 1974, p. 77.
3. Case contributed by Ron Seniska.
4. Melba Colgrove, Harold H. Bloomfield, and Peter McWilliams, *How to Survive the Loss of a Love* (New York: Bantam Books, 1976), p. 34.
5. Dawson, p. 4.
6. *Ibid.*, p. 5.
7. Colgrove, Bloomfield, and McWilliams, p. 28.
8. *Ibid.*, p. 64.

chapter eight
REBOUNDING FROM ILLNESS AND INJURY

Illness and injury have their obvious physical hardships. You feel terrible, you look terrible, you cough, you can't climb stairs, and you may lose some of your hair. For most forms of illness and injury, proper medical attention combined with the body's natural homeopathic tendencies, leads to recovery. Often the psychological aspects of illness are more difficult to overcome. A 6'4" man who fell off his ranch-style house while cleaning out the gutters put it this way,

> It's been the most uncomfortable period of my life. Imagine a big guy like myself with a leg cast and two arm casts. My both wrists were broken along with my left ankle. The doctors and nurse assured me my injuries would heal within a normal period of time. I believed them, but it didn't stop my inner turmoil. Imagine asking your wife to brush your teeth for you or zip down your fly so you can use the bathroom.

> Adding to the misery was explaining the accident incident to so many hundreds of people. How many times can you smile when somebody inquires about the accident and how it occurred. People should know better.

> Another disturbing aspect of being temporarily crippled is that I felt I wasn't carrying my share of the load. The insurance company was giving me my paycheck. My wife and kids were doing all my share of the household errands. I couldn't even drive myself to the doctor's for a check up. Little old ladies were opening doors for me. I felt so helpless and inadequate.

To make matters worse, I felt foolish for having fallen off my roof. I couldn't take that disapproving look in my wife's eyes. To tell you the truth, my life was a mess for too long a period of time. I still don't think I've fully recovered.

Recovering or rebounding from the emotional side effects of illness and injury isn't easy. But the grit and determination displayed by some of the people whom you will read about in this chapter provide some sharp insights into useful coping strategies.

GET EMOTIONAL SUPPORT
FROM A LOVED ONE

A strikingly consistent finding among people who have bounced back is that the emotional support of a family member helped them pull through the adversity. The therapeutic value of emotional closeness is illustrated by the coping of Ken, a burn victim. He recounts those agonizing days of his past:

> January, eight years ago, while engaged in the construction of an Urban Development Corporation Townhouse Project, I suffered major burns to over forty percent of my body. I was the victim of a fluke explosion that you think will never happen to you.
>
> The timing could not have been worse from a financial standpoint. My wife had given birth that very morning to our third child. We had closed on a new home in the suburbs three weeks previous, and we had not yet sold our other house. It was unbelievable. We had all at once two mortgages and the interim financing payments to worry about. Plus all the normal expenses of living and raising a family. Since the accident occurred at work, I would receive a maximum of $95 per week. At that time my normal weekly pay check was better than three times that.
>
> The initial prognosis was that I would be hospitalized for between nine months and a year. I was told that I would probably never walk again, assuming I lived. I was given a fifteen percent chance of surviving forty-eight hours. Two weeks later, I was still alive. As often happens to burn victims, I developed a blood infection. My demise seemed to be just around the corner, so the doctors and nurses thought.
>
> My recovery, by all established standards, was miraculous. After six

weeks in intensive care, and four weeks in a private room, I was allowed to go home. During the following five years, I became a regular at the hospital. I've lost count of the number of skin grafts I had to endure. But each operation was less complicated than those preceding it. So each was easier to take. To me, the I.V. bottle was about as routine as a sixpack of beer might be to the ordinary guy.

I think I know why I pulled through and lead a normal life today. I have always had a positive attitude. I believe that something good can come from any bad situation. Normally, I look for that good. I have never been one to dwell on the negative side, but rather to take the bull by the horns and turn things around.

Most of my good fortune since the accident, and the primary reason for my recovery, is my wife. She gave me the will to live. Anytime she came to see me, she had a cheerful voice and a smile. We had always been a team before. She was determined we would be an even better team after the accident. She would not accept any negative thoughts about my recovery. Not for a minute did she believe that I would not recover.

Our faith in each other, and our faith in God, has had the effect of making us believe that together we can do anything. By the work together, I do not mean the state of being constant companions. Rather that each of us has the one hundred percent support of the other. We never argue, and very seldom disagree. Each of us is sensitive to the other's concerns.

We did not know how we would get through the period described, but we knew we would. Too many things have happened to recall it all. I think the prime force which has helped us has been our ability to look for the bright side. With my wife at my side and on my side, I was always able to find a little bit of good every day. Neither of us was ever satisfied until we found the bright side of things. Determination and the love of my wife pulled me through.

I've come a long way from my close scrape with death. Today I have plans to open a consulting engineering firm of my own. Encouragement from my wife is going to help me achieve that goal, too.[1]

As mentioned several times previously, the psyche seems to crave support and reassurance from others when we are in physical or emotional difficulty. Thus, "Get Emotional Support from a Loved One" is particularly effective because the support comes from someone close to you rather than a stranger.

TRY DETERMINATION

Ken attributed part of his recovery to determination, as do many people who rebound from substantial illness or injury. The same spirit that enables people to stave off death also seems to be helpful in overcoming substantial physical ailments. If you try to rehabilitate yourself for a specific reason, you will be more successful than if you simply want to get better for the sake of your general well-being. The underlying chemistry might be that adrenaline and related hormones are more readily energized when your brain focuses on something specific. A computer operator in her late fifties tells an engaging story illustrating the value of focused determination.

> I had a terrible misfortune four years ago. I work for the Transportation Department. My husband, a bookkeeper, and I were coming home from work. It was about 5 P.M. and we stopped for a little shopping. We take the same route every day and that day was no different. We sat waiting in line to make our left turn off a busy boulevard.
>
> Like a bolt of lightning, a car driven by a woman slammed into us. The next thing I knew I was waking up in the intensive care unit of a hospital. I became heartsick when it was explained to me that I had shattered my leg in three places along with tearing a good portion of my calf muscle away from my leg. The injury was bad enough, but I was also told that my chances of walking again were three in ten.
>
> It hit me that I wouldn't be able to walk down the aisle with my family at my son Neal's wedding. His wedding was planned to be held in Michigan, his wife's hometown. The wedding was only eight months away. I shopped around at different doctors and physical therapists only to hear the same diagnosis: "You won't be able to walk again. All you can do is exercise the good leg so it won't go stiff." I exercised the good leg, but I was getting more and more frustrated as time went by. The wedding was getting closer, and I was getting more depressed about not being able to walk down the aisle.
>
> One Friday when I was alone in the house, I wondered why I could not exercise my injured leg, making it stronger. When my husband came home, I discussed with him the idea of exercising my leg. He agreed and proceeded to rig up a pulley with a strap on one end for my ankle and a canvas bag of lead weights on the other. I began with lighter weights at first. In four weeks I was up to eighteen pounds, lifting it sixty-five times a day. From that point, the

weight didn't increase, but I increased the number of times I lifted the weight.

About five weeks before the wedding, I called my therapist and asked him to come to the house right after dinner. When he arrived, I asked everyone to come into the den. I could tell that they were all puzzled. Then one of the happiest moments in my life took place. I arose and walked across the room using only a cane. Everyone was thrilled, especially me.

I was determined to walk down the aisle. And I did.[2]

Although this woman's story has been authenticated, one aspect might reflect a slight distortion of memory. A physical therapist would ordinarily encourage the exercising of the injured leg. The exercise rig her husband put together may have been suggested by her therapist and/or physician. The major point of the anecdote is that this courageous woman mobilized her energy to overcome her handicap in order to be able to walk at her son's wedding.

"Try Determination" might be an effective strategy for bouncing back because it is tied in with raising your level of expectation. If you are determined enough to accomplish something, it sometimes becomes a self-fulfilling prophecy.

BE OBSTINATE

The woman depicted in the previous section facilitated her partial recovery from illness by trying to accomplish a specific skill (walking) by a specific date (her son's wedding). Many other people attribute their ability to fight off illness to their obstinate attitude toward their affliction. Their refusal to surrender to the disease helps them combat the disease process. It obviously does not work for everybody, but obstinacy prolongs the survival of many people.

Shirley, a nurse, is an example of this principle in action. She was accustomed to human tragedy, having worked eighteen years in the emergency room of a small hospital. One day it was Shirley's turn for tragedy. Medical tests showed conclusive evidence that the severe headaches and vision problems she was experiencing were the result of a tumor on her brain stem. Shirley's physical condition deteriorated to the point that she was forced to retire. Although a determined and devoted worker, she no longer had the mental concentration and physical stamina to properly care for patients.

Forced retirement was a difficult blow for Shirley to absorb. The next blow was worse. Her doctors informed her that she had less than two years to live. Shirley did not dispute the doctors' verdict, but she refused to accept it. The brain-stem tumor had taken away her professional career, but she decided she wasn't going to let it end her life. Shirley developed an obstinate, defiant attitude that she still lives by today, five years after the fatal diagnosis.[3]

"Be Obstinate" can be viewed as a combination of establishing a difficult goal for yourself and using a positive mental attitude to achieve that goal. It will work for you in many adverse situations.

COMPENSATE

An eminently realistic strategy for many injury victims is to find a substitute activity. An extreme example of this type was a dentist who caught his hand in a snow blower. Shortly after his return to practice, the dentist decided to retire. Although his license had not been revoked, he deemed himself unfit to perform some of the delicate maneuvers required of a dentist. He worried more about the welfare of his patients than his personal income and status.

The compensatory activity that the dentist chose was to pursue his hobby, cabinet and furniture making, for a living. He states, "My hands are good enough for working with wood. If I make a small mistake I can only ruin some wood. As a dentist, one small mistake could do permanent damage to a facial nerve. I'll get by as a carpenter. A big income isn't everything."

Compensation is often an effective method of bouncing back from an athletic injury. Chuck, a high school athlete, faced such a situation. His closest friend describes it this way:

> Chuck was an incredible high school athlete. Basing a career on this ability, Chuck planned to become a physical education major at college. He hoped to earn a football scholarship in order to pay for a major part of his expenses.

Chuck encountered some misfortune in the next to last football game during his senior year. On a routine play, he was hit from the side, tearing cartilage and tendons in his knee. As a result of the injury, Chuck was operated on two days later. Half of the cartilage in the knee was removed. After the injury and operation, his athletic career ended. Along with his athletic career went his hopes for a scholarship and an education at a large four-year college.

After the operation, Chuck was depressed, but started to realize his accident might have been a blessing in disguise. Even though Chuck did not have the finances to go to a big college, he worked part-time and attended a two-year community college. Chuck did not give up on sports completely. He has become a certified football and baseball umpire, and also films high school games for the coaching staff.

As a result of his accident and subsequent limp, Chuck re-evaluated his career goals. In his search to investigate whether or not he could obtain a physical education degree, Chuck learned that it was tough to find a job as a physical education teacher. Learning of this situation, Chuck began to take business courses and work at his family's hardware store where he seemed to have a future.[4]

Chuck thus made a double compensation in order to rebound from his hope-shattering injury. He found a substitute way to enjoy athletics by becoming an umpire and a sports photographer. He also appears to have found a substitute career in working for a family business rather than pursuing his goal of becoming a coach and physical education teacher.

"Compensate" is a direct example of using a defense mechanism to your advantage when coping with adversity. It also provides the theoretical basis for the strategy described next.

CONCENTRATE ON ANOTHER ASPECT OF YOURSELF

A form of compensation is concentrating on another aspect of yourself, in order to cope with a serious injury or illness. For example, a construction worker might receive a bad back injury. Instead of spending his lifetime bemoaning his fate, he could concentrate on his intellectual side and perhaps become a bookkeeper or computer programmer. Prior to the change in his life, this construction worker might have perceived himself as the outdoors type who finds office work distasteful. As his new self-image develops, he successfully rebounds from his back injury.

Clarence, a sales manager today, describes the circumstances under which he had to concentrate on another aspect of himself in order to survive:

> Reminiscing, I find myself back five years ago. I was in excellent health, an all-around athlete, and my future looked bright. I had never been seriously ill nor hurt in my life nor had I ever needed anyone. I was a natural leader, and always on top of situations. After leaving home at seventeen, and finishing high school on my own, I found employment in an aircraft plant. I took an immediate liking to machinery, so I stuck with it.
>
> During one period, I was working the 3:30 P.M. to midnight shift. One night after leaving work, I decided that I would take a different route home, a route without traffic lights. At 12:45 A.M. I was sideswiped by another car. I was thrown from my car through the driver's window. In the process of being thrown through the window, I hit the steering wheel with such an impact that my spleen ruptured and my right lung collapsed.
>
> I was given a fifty percent chance of survival. I spent eight hours in the operating room. Two days later, I woke up in the intensive care unit, to find my parents and baby brother by my side. After learning about my physical condition, I had no choice but to accept it and begin the long road back. The trip would be difficult, but I was determined I would not be defeated.
>
> I recovered remarkably fast, but I knew I would never be the same again. My physical condition had deteriorated and I had lost forty pounds. I hated to have to accept help from so many people. Realizing that my superior physical days were finished, I decided that the best way to deal with the situation was to concentrate on the intellectual me. I began the painful process of starting night school. Thus ended the old life, and a new one began. Now and then I long for the other me, that strong dude who could do no wrong. I long for the other me, but I know I can never return to yesterday, so I go forward.[5]

"Concentrate on Another Aspect of Yourself" is similar to compensation, but it is more accurately labelled *substitution*. You substitute one activity for one that is no longer a possibility. The substitution makes life much more bearable.

PERSEVERE IN YOUR USUAL ACTIVITIES

For some people, compensation, or emphasizing a new aspect of themselves, is not the best antidote to coping with a serious injury. Instead, they return to their normal way of life despite their disability. Defying the odds brings them comfort. Thus the jogger who experiences a mild heart attack returns to jogging as soon as possible. The psychotherapist who loses her vision in an accident continues the practice of psychotherapy. The bowler who loses a finger in a buzz-saw accident returns to bowling using a modified bowling ball.

Elaine represents a glowing example of how a return to normal activities can be the treatment of choice. At age thirty-one, Elaine was the mother of a nine-year-old son, an active tennis player and swimmer, and a successful realtor. Her husband called her, affectionately, the Blonde Dynamo. While on vacation in Bermuda, Elaine was involved in a serious moped accident. She was thrown thirty feet from her vehicle. Her right leg was so badly mangled that it had to be amputated about six inches above the knee.

Her long road back is a story of determination and courage. She was helped by an orthopedic team from the hospital, an exercise rehabilitation program, and the encouragement of her husband and son. She was fitted with a prosthetic device that clings to the upper thigh by suction. Using this advanced technique, she did not require a belt. She describes:

> Lying in the hospital, I had dreadful thoughts of never leading a normal life again. I had worked so many years trying to develop my tennis game. Gone forever in one stupid accident. Also down the drain was my fabulous career as a realtor. Who would buy a home from a woman hobbling around on one leg? I was completely irrational.
>
> Soon after I returned home, I began to develop a sensible attitude about my disability. All those irrational thoughts in the hospital were just irrational. No one ever said that a woman with a prosthesis couldn't sell houses, play tennis, or swim, raise a son, or make love to her husband.

The doctors said I was a wonderful healer. My rehab specialists said at the rate I was going, I'd be climbing stairs in no time. I did return to work some fifteen months later. I navigated stairs with the best of them. My sales climbed back to normal. Swimming was relatively easy after I overcame the embarrassment of swimming with my prosthetic device left behind in the locker room.

Tennis was the most complicated part of my recovery program. I decided to switch from singles to doubles because it's just too much to cover an entire court with only one natural leg. In the past, I was a ladies "A" player. I switched, becoming a strong "B" player. I presently play in long white slacks, the style of years ago, rather than shorts.

I feel pretty good these days. I think if I had given up on my career, my tennis, and my swimming, I would be one demoralized lady. Instead, I'm just about the Blonde Dynamo I used to be, if you overlook my occasional hobble.

"Persevere in Your Usual Activities" is a healthy form of the defense mechanism, denial. Elaine was aware that she had lost a leg, but she denied that it would prevent her from ever playing tennis again. Denial, requiring strong will, can aid you in overcoming physical handicaps.

DO YOUR BEST TO LEAD
A NORMAL LIFE

A severe illness or injury sometimes leaves the person faced with a major philosophical dilemma: to fit into the mainstream or not to fit into the mainstream? In other words, despite your disability, should you participate as fully as possible in the world of people who do not share your disability or should you segregate yourself by involving yourself as much as possible with others with the same affliction? Several professional-level workers who are handicapped believe that mainstreaming is the best solution. So does a blind man who holds an executive position. Bruce Rider, the Community Action Manager at Xerox Corporation, was granted a social leave of absence from his company to work as the director of employment at a local chapter of the Association for the Blind. His perceptions about blindness and blind workers provide insight into the problems and opportunities of many handicapped workers. The following is an excerpt from a newspaper article:

Bruce Rider wouldn't advise a blind person to become a bus driver or a brain surgeon. But beyond a few occupations in which sight is essential, he sees no limit to what a blind person can do.

"There's only one thing you can say about being blind—we don't see stuff," Rider says. "Blind people can be fat or thin, sloppy or neat, bright or dull. Blind means you can't see and that's the only generality you can make."

"I want to do two things," Rider says. "I want to find blind people who want jobs or better jobs. And I want to show the business world that blind people are people—to alleviate some of the ignorance. An employer can't look at me and tell me a blind person can't work."

Seven years ago, Rider was an up–and–coming young salesman for Xerox in Charleston, S.C., when he began to lose his sight (because of a rare visual disease). Vision in his left eye was totally destroyed. He still has some peripheral vision in his right eye enabling him to read large print on a closed circuit television set designed for the blind. He gets around with the use of a guide dog.

"I live in two worlds—the normal world and the handicapped world," Rider says. "The tension that exists between the two is overwhelming. I have seen the resistance of employers to hiring handicapped people. Now I'm discovering a lot of blind people are no longer willing to participate in the sighted world. I'm guessing they are tired of rejection."

The result is that handicapped people tend to be segregated.

"I would like to talk to people about what it is like to live in the mainstream," Rider says. "At least, I can tell them what my life is like and describe some of the risks. I'm not saying everybody has to go into the mainstream. It's a hard thing. There is safety in segregation. It's almost like being in jail. At least, you know the routine."

Rider says blind people who have never held a job will have special problems just as women do when they re-enter the job market after many years in the home. He has worked all his life and hopes to help them by sharing his work experiences.

"One reason there is so much ignorance about how to deal with the handicapped is the tendency to hide them away," Rider says.

Society likes to pretend everyone is young and beautiful and healthy—or should be. "When you see ads, you never see old people or handicapped people," Rider says. "We must begin to show people role models. In reality there are no perfect people. You are who you are and that's okay. I have never been willing to let others define me."[6]

"Do Your Best to Lead a Normal Life" is closely tied in with two basic psychological concepts: preservation of self-esteem and raising your expectations. For many handicapped people, "mainstreaming" helps preserve their self-esteem. Raising expectations fits in because the handicapped person who expects to function in a non-handicapped world will find ways to do so.

DEVELOP EMPATHY FOR OTHERS

Developing empathy for others can help you cope with your physical illness or injury. Developing new insights into the problems of others becomes a positive spin-off from your own misfortunes. Dr. M. Richard Rose, a college president and former top-level government advisor, is one person who believes strongly in this coping strategy.

Dr. Rose was involved in a motorcylce accident one summer as he and his four friends were on their way from New York State to Maine. While riding down a mountain road near Lincoln Gap, Vermont, Rose's motorcycle slid out of control in some gravel spread on a horseshoe curve.

"I saw what I thought was a meadow," recalls Dr. Rose. "I thought I would roll out into the meadow rather than sliding all the way around the corner." What he thought was a meadow proved to be an optical illusion. It was the top of a grove of trees. "As soon as the front wheel went over, I knew I was in serious trouble."

Dr. Rose fell about thirty feet and fractured his left thigh bone. He managed to tie his boot laces together and wrap his belt around his knees, using his right leg as a splint for his left. Dr. Rose then hotwired his motorcycle horn to alert passing motorists to his location.

At that time, his friends realized his absence and came back to find Dr. Rose. The college president was rushed to the Burlington

Medical Center where he underwent surgery the next day. He spent eight days at the medical center and two more days in a hospital back in the town where he lived and worked. It took about one year for an almost complete recovery. At that point, Rose, an avid runner, was back doing some running. Within that year, his limp had vanished.

A positive outcome of his accident, according to Dr. Rose, is the greater appreciation he has of what it means to be permanently handicapped. "I have a deeper understanding of what handicapped people have to cope with in terms of distance, crowded elevators and heavy doors," he explains.[7]

"Develop Empathy for Others" ties in with an interesting concept called *functional analysis*. One of its implications is that almost any event has some unintended positive and negative consequences. To bounce back, your job is to look for the unintended positive consequences. By empathizing with others when you are in trouble, you develop some new understandings that make you a fuller person.

FIND A LESS STRENUOUS SITUATION

Elaine, the courageous amputee depicted in a previous section, resolved some of her recovery problems by playing in a lesser league. Instead of playing women's "A" singles, she shifted down to women's "B" doubles. The same principle of playing in a lesser league can be helpful in a variety of situations.

An example of this strategy is Ray, a man with a hard-driving personality. As a sales manager in a New York City-based textile company, he had good reason to be impatient and demanding. As do many other Type A personalities, he experienced a heart attack. Following his doctor's orders and the pleas of his wife, Ray found a slightly less competitive situation in which to live and work. His company rewarded him with a comfortable sales territory in Miami and surrounding areas. He enjoyed his relationships with customers and the opportunity to relax on the beach. One year later at a company meeting, he told his former co-workers, "Glad to leave the rat race behind. I'm making a living and I'm alive to enjoy it."

Another example is Gerry, a free lance magazine photographer, who was making an enviable living. He led a life of high adventure, shooting photos on assignments such as covering motor racing events, civil uprisings, and the weddings of monarchs. Misfortune befell Gerry as he developed a neuromuscular disorder that was difficult both to diagnose and treat. This disease made walking very painful for Gerry. Toting photography equipment around airports and maneuvering around crowds became too much for Gerry's limited mobility. The less strenuous activity that he chose was to open a small photo studio. His high adventure now consisted of shooting babies, weddings, pets, bar mitzvahs and bos mitzvahs. Gerry liked the fact that his shift in occupations allowed him to reduce his daily pain.

"Find a Less Strenuous Situation" is yet another example of realistic goal setting. Elaine wisely shifted from her tennis playing to a more realistic level, considering her permanent disability. Ray and Gerry, too, established some realistic goals, and made comebacks from discouraging situations.

LEARN TO TOLERATE LITTLE FAILURES

One of the major roadblocks to emotionally recovering from illness and injury is to learn to accept little failures. When you learn to accept minor inconveniences, you are better able to cope with physical setbacks. Selma, a young grandmother, developed arthritis. As the arthritis grew in intensity, she accepted the fact that her hands would not be as pretty as they once were. Selma also learned to accept the frequent pain. What she couldn't accept at first were the little failures that seemed to pop up daily. She explains it this way,

> What hurt me more than anything was not being able to do well the little things that I used to do routinely. I take care of my granddaughter quite frequently during the day because her mother works. Tracy, my granddaughter, likes me to do things for her. One day she wanted me to lace up her roller skates real tight. Well, I just couldn't do it. Another time she expected me to shorten a pair of her jeans. I couldn't do that either because my fingers were hurting so much that day. She cried one day because I couldn't braid her hair the way I used to.

Selma's turnaround came about when she finally learned to accept the fact that little failures were an inevitable part of her disease.

> It finally grabbed me that today's failures will not necessarily be repeated tomorrow. Some days my arthritis flares up worse than on other days. If I'm having a bad spell, it doesn't mean that tomorrow will be bad too. I learned to tell Tracy that my hands would be well enough next week to help her out. She learned to believe me.

> Tracy is beginning to learn that there are times she will have to help me. The other day I sent her to next door to ask the neighbor to open an applesauce jar for us. I couldn't manipulate the jar and neither could Tracy. It's not the end of the world. It's just the way life is when you're an arthritic. My problems are small in comparison to others.

"Learn to Tolerate Little Failures" is, at a deeper level, modifying your self-concept in a realistic direction. You have to accept the fact that due to some forms of illness and injury you are not exactly the same person you were in the past.

OVERCOME YOUR DEPENDENCE ON OTHERS

The psychological aspects of illness and injury are difficult to overcome until the injured person learns to shake the dependencies established during the early stages of infirmity. Being bed-ridden, chair-ridden, or even house-ridden, makes you dependent upon others. The disabled person often makes requests for small favors, such as changing television channels or taking a plate into the kitchen.

If you are incapacitated, these dependencies become a natural way of life. Such dependencies lead to despondencies, unless you can break the cycle or have somebody else be courageous enough to force you to become independent again. An important part of bouncing back from illness or injury is to act maturely and become self-sufficient. Graham, an attorney, was a stroke victim. He survived, but his rehabilitation process was slow. As many other stroke victims do, he developed a "stroke personality," which involves considerable dependency upon others.[8] His wife, Kathy, describes how she helped him function better:

Graham used to be the most resourceful guy. Sometimes I felt somewhat inadequate in our relationship because he expected so little from me. Once he suffered the stroke, all that was reversed. He became almost too dependent on me. In the early days of his recovery, I had to even do things like mop the drool from his chin. I was also expected to find his slippers, his comb, his wallet, or whatever he left around. I ran all his errands.

As Graham's physical rehabilitation improved, his mental attitude improved, but not at the same rate. He still expected too much from me. Gradually I began to suggest that he do things for himself such as getting the newspaper from the front porch, setting the alarm clock, or paying the monthly bills. I also encouraged him to take the initiative about deciding whether or not we should go out on a Saturday. Before his stroke, he always took the initiative on such things.

When I changed my willingness to help him with everything, Graham at first thought I was rejecting him. Then he began to realize that by not overindulging him anymore, I was actually helping him. From that point, his recovery proceeded much more swiftly. Within a couple of months, he was working parttime at his law practice.

"Overcome Your Dependence on Others" is self-explanatory from a theoretical standpoint. An injured person will develop heightened dependency needs. In order to facilitate recovery, these dependency needs will have to gradually diminish. A gradual withdrawal is recommended.

STOP BEING A FISHPERSON

A frequent negative byproduct of serious illness or injury is that the person develops into a chronic complainer. The complaining is in reality a symptom of the depressive aspects of being confined to the house or apartment. As the infirmed individual's daily complaints mount, the willingness of family members to give that person encouragement and support decreases. With less encouragement and support, the complaints escalate further.

The complaints of the illness or accident victim can be about almost anything. Some are directly related to the illness, such as grumbling about misfortune and personal misery. Other complaints take the form of self-pity. To facilitate recovery from physical misfortune, something has to be done to break the cycle of depressed feelings. These feelings lead to whining and complaining, which leads to more depression.

The wife of a stroke victim explains how she confronted him with his complaining to achieve a turnaround in his behavior: "When Clay started complaining regularly, I told him I realized what a 'fishwife' is. It has nothing to do with gender. It's a syndrome of the person left alone at home with not enough to do, and feeling depressed. After that, he stopped being a fishperson much of the time."[9]

If you can slip out of the trap of being a fishperson you might be on the road to recovering from your infirmity.

"Stop Being a Fishperson" relates to the defense mechanism, *acting out.* Flooded with the anxiety surrounding an illness, it is natural to lash out at others which is a direct form of acting out.

NOTES

1. Case researched by Thomas A. Guerin.
2. Case researched by Arthur Robin.
3. Case researched by Richard M. Thompson.
4. Case researched by Leslie Payne.
5. Case researched by Clarence L. Baccus, Jr.
6. Source: Betty Utterback, "Blind to the Possibilities," Rochester *Democrat and Chronicle,* May 20, 1979, pp. C1–2.
7. Quote and details of story from "Rose Describes Recovery," *News and Events,* Rochester Institute of Technology, September 25, 1980, p. 5.
8. A full description of stroke personality is found in Charles Clay Dahlberg and Joseph Jaffe, *Stroke* (New York: W. W. Norton, 1977).
9. Quoted in a *Psychology Today* excerpt from *Stroke,* June 1977, p. 126.

chapter nine
COPING WITH JOB REVERSALS

Many successful people have experienced some type of job reversal. A distinguishing characteristic of these individuals is their capacity to roll with the punches and live through the time of trouble with a minimum of fret, confusion, and disorientation. The career-minded person who rants, raves, or throws a temper tantrum when things don't go well is paving the way for even harder times ahead. Nobody always wins on the job. At one time or another, most people will be passed over for a promotion, demoted, criticized, abandoned by a favorite subordinate, or fired.

In this chapter field-tested tactics will be described for handling job reversals other than being fired.[1] Many of the tactics (and attitudes) also can be used upon being fired. Firing is such a major life trauma that it will be discussed separately in the following chapter and touched upon lightly in this one. As with any place in this book, if a particular strategy or tactic looks appropriate for dealing with a situation other than the one it was designed to handle, give it a try. Many strategies can be helpful for dealing with a variety of problems.

DISCOVER THE FACTS BEHIND YOUR DEFEAT

When you are demoted, passed over, fired, or subject to any other significant job reversal, you owe it to yourself to find out why. Discovering the facts behind your setback is the logical way to learn from your mistakes. Usually, you have to calm down sufficiently to assume this objective, problem-solving posture. Getting an accurate answer may not always be easy, but the facts could help you avoid a similar setback at a later date. Despite all that has been preached in recent years about the importance of honesty and openness in management, you may still have to probe to get an authentic answer as to why you were defeated. Gary, passed over for a managerial promotion, did just that.

How can I tell my wife, he thought to himself. It's the third time that I have been passed over for a regional managership. Each time, the company told me that I would be warmly considered for the next promotion. Gary's reflection was followed by sullenness and then finally by action. He demanded a conference with his boss, Elmer, to discuss why he was passed over again. With some hesitation, Elmer did agree to review the reasons why Gary was not selected for the position of regional manager.

> "Your work performance has been fine," began Elmer. "It's just a few little things that made us decide to give somebody else a chance this time around. It's not too much to worry about."
>
> "Elmer, that is precisely why I came to see you. It *is* something to worry about. Is there something holding me back in the company? I must know. Maybe it's something I can correct. What are these little things you refer to?"
>
> "Gary, this may hurt, but you asked for it. My boss and I think you are rude to top management. It's this rudeness that is keeping you back."
>
> "I don't recall being rude to anybody. Could you give me a couple of examples?"
>
> "The best example I can think of is when Mr. Finney, the executive vice-president, joined us for lunch. When we were returning from lunch, you barged through the revolving door ahead of him. During his presentation you clipped your nails. Just like you do in other meetings, you interrupted him before he had a chance to finish what he was saying. Do you get the point? We think you need more polish."

Gary thought the company was being needlessly picayune, but now he had a clear understanding of what aspects of his behavior were holding him back. Gary could quit in a huff or conform to what the company thought constituted good manners in dealing with those in higher management. By taking the latter course of action, Gary's hopes of becoming a regional manager were reignited. At no sacrifice to his sense of morality, Gary did become more deferent toward higher-ranking executives. Fourteen months later, a new region was formed and Gary was selected to become a regional manager.

"Discover the Facts Behind Your Defeat" is a self-explanatory application of clarifying the problem. Simultaneously you benefit from the feedback associated with gathering these facts.

WELCOME THAT ROCK-BOTTOM FEELING

A philosophical, as well as a psychological, way of coping with job reversals is to be happy when you hit rock bottom. Once you accept the fact that things cannot get worse, you are mentally prepared for a comeback. Oddly enough, the stress of things being so bad that they can only improve sometimes brings on a temporary euphoria. One explanation is that people laugh at how bad things are as a way of relieving tension.

When you are truly convinced that your problems have bottomed out, you are preparing yourself emotionally for a recovery. That "nothing-else-can-go-wrong" feeling helps you mobilize your energy to begin your counterattack.

Winfred, a small company president, has used this strategy on more than one occasion. The spirit of optimism that underlies his rock-bottom strategy has pulled his company through hard times on more than one occasion. To illustrate, one day Winfred turned to his secretary and said,

> Cheer up, Mary. It looks like we have finally hit the bottom of the barrel. From now on, things are going to get better. We have laid off half of our work force, our business has shrunk 45 percent this year, and our new computerized order system has caused us endless problems.
>
> The future looks better. Business conditions are improving, and the people in the company are mostly our better employees. It's a good feeling to know that things won't get any worse.

Stock market investors have used this rock-bottom strategy for many years. An experienced investor attempts to purchase stock at its lowest point. To that investor, something hitting bottom is a signal of good news (assuming the prediction about bottoming out is correct).

"Welcome that Rock-Bottom Feeling" is indirectly related to developing a positive mental attitude. Once you are convinced that things cannot get worse, you are prepared to begin thinking positively about the future.

SALVAGE YOUR MISTAKES

A handy middle-aged man constructed his own built-in swimming pool despite the admonitions of his wife and two close friends. His cement pool was esthetically sound, but structurally unsound. During its first winter it developed two massive cracks. Feeling temporarily defeated, and somewhat humiliated, he originally decided to remove the pool. His substitute course of action was to fill the pool with dirt and make a flower garden, a choice that received the spirited cooperation of his wife. The enjoyment he and his wife now derive from the flower garden exceeds the enthusiasm they had for the pool during its brief period of functioning.

On-the-job mistakes are not as easily salvaged as an improperly constructed pool, but the underlying principle remains the same. Salvage what you can from a job reversal. At times an imaginative solution will be required to complete the salvage operation. Craig, an ambitious twenty-nine-year old, worked as a financial analyst for a large company. Having heard much about the importance of being well-rounded in order to become an executive, he pulled strings to obtain a transfer to the marketing research department. Both Craig and his new boss were quite pleased with the result. Craig was making a contribution to his new department and obtaining valuable experience in the process.

Then came the budget crunch. Layoffs were announced throughout the company. Craig's boss told him that since he was the last hired into the department, he would have to be the first fired. Craig's old boss informed him that there was a freeze on adding anymore people to the financial division. Craig then went back to his marketing boss, asking if there was anything at all he could do to stay in the market research department or marketing division. His boss told Craig, "The only thing I know of is a sales territory in the north country. They just lost their fourth sales rep this year. Go speak to the sales manager with my blessing." (The sales department in Craig's company was part of the marketing division.)

Craig was told he could have the sales territory but at a twenty percent reduction in pay. Craig reasoned that the job would give him good experience, and that the income he received from the job would be better than no income. Craig endured in the job for two years at which point he was offered a position as a supervisor of financial analysis. The manager of the financial division of the company reasoned that Craig was more valuable than ever. His sales experience in a tough territory had made his financial judgment more astute. Craig had truly salvaged his mistake of having transferred into a job that lasted only a few months. Many people would have quit in disgust rather than patiently working out a solution to the prospects of being laid off.

"Salvage Your Mistakes" is a constructive use of the defense mechanism, *substitution.* You substitute one position (or activity) for another, with the hope of achieving a higher position in the future.

DON'T BE A HOTHEAD

A good way to compound your losses is to overreact to a reversal by being a hothead or sore loser. Blair, a product manager, thought he had a wonderful idea for a new product line for his company, instant home fries. He put together some facts and figures about the new generation of two-paycheck families that were looking for attractive new instant foods. Since home fries could be served with a variety of brunches and dinners, and were more exciting than mashed potatoes, Blair was convinced he had a winner.

The new product committee, however, had different thoughts. Although they could see the merit in marketing instant home fries, they

thought the project was too risky. A major negative factor, the committee thought, was the fact that instant mashed potatoes had failed for
other companies. Instead of home fries, the committee put their support behind expanding their line of low-calorie salad dressings.

Blair did not take rejection of his ideas gracefully. Instead, he
wrote several nasty memos to the company president and the head of
the new product committee. It seemed to some of Blair's immediate
subordinates that he was hoping for the new line of salad dressings to
fail, in order to prove that the company had made the wrong choice.

Several months later another division of the company was interested in interviewing Blair as a prospective marketing director, a
position made available by a sudden resignation. The division president
asked the president of Blair's division if he might have permission to
interview Blair. In addition, the other division president wanted to know
what Blair's president thought of him.

Permission was granted to interview Blair, but the reference was
not encouraging. The specific comment was, "Blair used to be a stable
guy and a team worker. But recently he's become very excitable and
stubborn. He doesn't know when to back off. Maybe it's personal problems." Blair's candidacy was dropped because of his hotheaded attitude about his home fry potatoes.

"Don't Be a Hothead" serves as a reminder that developing and
maintaining emotional control is a lifelong problem. Suppression
of emotion is not the answer, but it is helpful to find constructive
ways of displacing your emotion and feelings.

PERFORM WELL IN UNDESIRABLE ASSIGNMENTS

At higher job levels, there is a tendency to demote, rather than fire, an
individual who performs poorly or falls out of political favor. (At lower
levels, there is a greater probability that the employee with the falling
out will be asked to resign.) The practice of demoting a top-level employee to an undesirable assignment frequently serves to humiliate that
employee. It is often a wise choice for that employee to find a job with
another firm when receiving such a demotion. However, there is value

in weathering the situation, especially when the demotion was intended to belittle the employee. If the employee performs well on the bad assignment, respect and a good reputation will be gained within the firm.

Art, a computer project leader, was cognizant of the importance of performing well in a lesser assignment. Art had developed the reputation of being a superior project leader, and was considered in line for a promotion. Somehow, the new vice-president in his area did not think highly of Art. Through the new VP's influence, Art was reassigned to a mediocre staff job as a committee organizer. Art would not let this unofficial demotion get the better of him. He did an exemplary job in his new position. Gradually the new vice-president changed his perception of Art, and he was eventually promoted to a position higher than his old level.[2]

"Perform Well in Undesirable Assignments" illustrates the importance of avoiding self-defeating behavior. Performing poorly in an undesirable assignment will only defeat your long-range purpose of rebuilding your career while standing firm and overcoming the humiliation of the demotion will gain you respect from others.

MOVE OUT OF THE GRAVEYARD AS SOON AS POSSIBLE

Art's strategy of staying put in his new assignment and performing well obviously worked. In other situations, the best strategy is to find a quiet way out of a *graveyard* assignment. There is a nuance of difference between an undesirable assignment and a graveyard. Many positions may be undesirable but a graveyard position is clearly a dead end job. A sound strategy is to earnestly try to be transferred away from a dead end assignment after you have made a sincere effort for a reasonable time to improve the situation.

A large corporation established a salvaging department staffed mainly by people with emotional and physical disabilities (such as people with cardiac problems who had been advised to avoid stress). From the outset, the department became known throughout the corporation as The Graveyard. Managers in the department were generally considered unpromotable.

Fifty-five-year old Judd was appointed, against his wishes, to a middle-manager position in the Graveyard. A friend in personnel gave Judd her honest opinion about the situation: "Judd, you've just about been put out to pasture. The only way you'll ever get out of this department is through retirement. But if you like that kind of work, your future is assured with the company. Besides, the people working there are stable and appreciative. You might feel like you're doing some good for them."

A vigorous man, Judd did not wish to see himself placed in a terminal position; however, he did enjoy the challenge of a salvage operation. He decided that he would stay in his graveyard position until he acquired enough knowledge about salvage operations to enter business for himself. Two years later, Judd, his brother-in-law, and a close friend established a small scrap metal business. His career was anew with excitement. Judd had bounced back from The Graveyard.

"Move Out of the Graveyard As Soon As Possible" is closely related to developing an action plan. It is important to develop a systematic plan to redevelop your career thrust.

TAKE ONE STEP BACKWARDS
TO GO TWO STEPS FORWARD

Since demotion is such a frequent form of job reversal it is worthwhile to consider one more potential strategy for handling it. Instead of feeling defeated by the demotion, it can be regarded as a valuable opportunity. Such was the case with Harry. Employed as an electrical design engineer, he failed to receive the promotion to senior design and project engineer that he had expected. Instead of being overwhelmed by the loss of the promotion, Harry quietly searched for a new position outside the firm. He landed a position with a new and rapidly-growing electronics firm which had just entered the market with several new products.

Because the new firm was investing so much money in new equipment, they were temporarily quite rigid about starting job grades and pay. Harry was forced to enter the firm as a technician, one full step below the job level of engineer. Because of his vast knowledge in electronic design, he was soon promoted to senior design engineer and project planning manager with the new firm. Within eighteen months after leaving the firm that denied him a promotion, Harry had more than made up for his temporary setback.[3]

"Take One Step Backwards to Go Two Steps Forward" might also be conceptualized as an action plan. In order to advance your career, you devise a method of taking on less responsibility temporarily in order to gain more responsibility in the long range.

HAVE AN ALTERNATE PLAN

Many people have problems coping with adversity, both on and off the job, because they fail to develop alternate plans in case the original plan goes astray. Such contingency planning is a normal part of business, but many people fail to develop contingency plans for themselves. This strategy of having an alternate plan can work for a company, too.

A well-known domestic manufacturer of industrial machinery survived foreign competition by establishing an alternate plan. Their main product became noncompetitive because two Japanese companies developed a duplicate version that sold for one-third less than the price of the well-known company. The alternate plan that the domestic company developed was to become a sub-contractor for other companies until they could find a new product of their own. By helping other companies with their overload, the machinery maker was able to avoid any substantial layoffs. Within three years, the company developed a new product, an industrial robot, that provided them an adequate level of business.

Sometimes a small, common-sense idea can prevent you from being setback by an unpredictable circumstance beyond your control. Such was George's experience. Several weeks prior to the company picnic, he was busy planning the activities for his co-workers. Wanting to make the picnic a success, he planned for athletic activities that are usually standard fare at picnics: volleyball, softball, badminton, croquet, and horseshoes. On the morning of the picnic, there was a slight shower, despite a forecast of generally clear weather. Realizing that weather forecasts aren't guarantees, George decided to plan activities in case of rain. His contingency plan was to borrow three sets of darts and dartboards which he placed in the trunk of his car.

By noon, most of the company's employees were at the picnic site. George welcomed all his co-workers and informed them of the activities he had planned for the day. The sky was a bit cloudy, but the picnic did not appear to be in danger of being washed out. One hour later, a few drops of rain began falling. The picnickers scurried to the log cabin for protection. George could hear the mutterings about the day being ruined, but instead of panicking, he ran for his contingency plan.

George's dart-game alternative was an immediate success. His biggest challenge was to dissuade the most inebriated of company employees to find something safer to do than hurl darts. His confidence bolstered by the success of his dart game, he suggested charades as another indoor activity, particularly for those people physically unfit for darts. The crowd liked the idea. By the end of the day, George was congratulated for having done an outstanding job of organizing the annual company picnic.

Although George's contingency planning is hardly consequential, it does illustrate how minor job-related reversals can be prevented. Few picnic organizers shine at a rainy picnic.

"Have an Alternate Plan" is referred to as *contingency planning* in the jargon of management. It is also a manifestation of finding creative alternatives. Having an alternative plan allows you options, from which you can choose the best plan.

REGROUP AND TRY AGAIN

A popular approach to dealing with job reversals affecting a group of people is to get back together in a huddle and try again. Thus the congressional committee, whose ideas are shot down out of committee, rethinks the proposal and submits it again. This "back to the drawing board" approach is so basic that some people neglect it when their initial efforts meet with resistance. Sometimes your ideas will be rejected largely because the time is not right for their acceptance. Regroup later, and the idea might click. Joanne and three of her friends had just such an experience.

Several years ago Joanne, an intelligent woman with modest formal education, found herself disappointed with her life style. A divorced mother, she found it quite unprofitable to work in an office and pay for child care services out of her meager earnings. She wanted more income and more flexible working hours. She approached two of her divorced friends who had children with her money-making idea:

> Let's go into the home-cleaning business. We'll call ourselves Tidy Women, Inc. We'll buy an old van and some household cleaning supplies. We'll need four women altogether to swing the deal. While three of us are cleaning somebody's house, the other one will stay at her home and care for all the pre-school children. She also can look out for the older kids after school. We'll take turns either cleaning or taking care of children. The pay has got to be better than office work, especially when you figure that we won't need as much clothing. We also won't have child-care expenses.

Joanne's friends were a little skeptical, but they thought they would at least give it a try. All agreed that it would be foolish to quit their jobs until they saw how business developed. Enough business did not develop to make Tidy Women, Inc. a worthwhile alternative to office jobs. Dismayed, but not crushed, Joanne and her friends decided to temporarily disband. Two years later, Joanne tried the idea again with two new team members. This time the idea caught on immediately. By the second time the business was tried, there were enough working couples in the community to make the effort pay off. Apparently Tidy Women had its largest potential market with two-paycheck families.

"Regroup and Try Again" is an obvious example of the importance of timing in business and personal life. A strategy that fails once may be of inherent value; it was simply implemented at a poor time. In the future, the same strategy might be a winner.

OVERCOME A PERSONAL DISQUALIFIER

Working on the weakness that created your setback, or that blocked your opportunity for moving forward, is another basic strategy. Unfortunately, too many people become defensive when confronted about a weakness or shortcoming that has held them back. Instead of overcoming the personal disqualifier, they aggravate the condition. One junior executive was denied a promotion. The reason offered was that he made very poor oral presentations. Instead of immediately taking action on his speaking ability, he quit in a huff.

Bill, a competent production worker, was able to overcome a personal disqualifier. He had worked for eight years on the line. His work was outstanding by his own evaluation and that of his bosses. To improve himself and qualify for a supervisory position, Bill enrolled in an evening program in a community college. He did quite well in his management and supervision program, achieving an A-minus average. An opportunity arose for a new shift supervisor position at the plant. Bill jumped at this opportunity for advancement.

After his interview, Bill felt confident. A week later, the new shift supervisor was named. Bill was infuriated that he was not the employee selected. Bill confronted the interviewer and asked for specific reasons for not receiving this promotion. Joe, the interviewer, leveled with Bill. "Even though your work record is good, you have some weaknesses that made it impossible for us to promote you to shift supervisor. You don't shave or shower enough. We get too many complaints about you from other workers. Good personal hygiene is an important part of a supervisor's job."

Angry, but not irrational, Bill left the confrontation session with one thing in mind. From now on, he would shave and shower regularly and wear clean clothing to the plant. Two months later Bill was told that he now carried a new image. Furthermore, he would be the logical contender for the next supervisory position.[4]

"Overcome A Personal Disqualifier" is an example of learning to confront your emotions and overcome defensive behavior. Learning to be open with your deficiencies takes practice, and for some people, cannot be done without the aid of professional help.

SWITCH TO THE WINNING TEAM

At times, you run into a career setback because you are assigned to a project or department whose overall performance is poor. Although you might be a standout performer on this losing team, other people's evaluation of you might be negatively biased because you are associated with a failure. Unfortunately, even your immediate superior might tend to give you a negative performance evaluation because the project to which you are assigned is doing poorly.

Jack, a mechanical engineer, was faced with this type of situation. He was assigned to work on an aircraft component with a history of performing poorly when it was placed under actual operating conditions. It seemed that every time he made a presentation about the product, he was forced to be the bearer of bad news. Despite his hard work and sincere effort, the performance evaluations were mediocre. Jack's break came when he was able to obtain a transfer to a fast-moving, successful product. Working as diligently as he did on the losing project, Jack began to obtain superior performance evaluations. He found it rewarding to work on the winning team.

The strategy of bouncing back from the negative impact of being associated with a losing effort has applicability beyond switching from one product to another. In most large businesses, there are winning departments and divisions. Similarly, government organizations have some agencies considered more effective than others. It takes patience and tact to switch to the winning team, but it can pay big dividends.

Another variation of joining the winning team is to leave a sponsor or mentor who has fallen into disfavor. One woman had spent three years cultivating one man as a sponsor. Gradually, the sponsor began to drink heavily in response to personal problems. As he drank more heavily, his personal problems intensified, leading to a continuation of the cycle. The woman disliked the idea of writing off all the time she had invested in her sponsor. But she also decided it would be advantageous to her career to not be associated with this troubled sponsor. As a first step in finding a new sponsor, she maneuvered her way onto a committee headed by a fast-moving woman in the firm. The committee head took a liking to the younger woman, and within six months the woman received a promotion to department supervisor.

Still another variation of switch to the winning team is the perennial favorite, "If you can't beat them, join them." A happy example is Harold, the operator of a small office and home cleaning service. A large outfit continually undercut his rates, finally forcing him out of business. Harold applied for, and received, a supervisory position with his predator. Three years later, he had worked his way up to vice-president, making twice the income he made when he had his own business.[5]

"Switch to the Winning Team" might be interpreted as a calculating way of taking care of your own interests. Instead of being concerned about the good of the organization, you put your self-interest first.

REALIZE YOU ARE ONE STEP CLOSER TO A SOLUTION

It is natural to become discouraged when your best efforts applied to a vexing problem do not lead to a solution. If you are to bounce back from this disparaging situation, you must have an attitude that will draw some good from the situation. You now have tested the idea and know that it must be improved.

The origins of this strategy trace at least as far back as Thomas Edison. He was once asked by a friend why he kept on trying to make a new type of battery, when he had failed so often. Edison replied: "Failure? I have no failures. Now I know fifty thousand ways it won't work."[6]

"Realize That You Are One Step Closer to a Solution" is another manifestation of developing a positive mental attitude. Despite temporary setbacks, you maintain an optimistic outlook toward the future.

CHANGE GOALS

A substantial amount of career frustration is attributable to not reaching goals that you think are important. If you can lower these goals or substitute new goals, without compromising your values, you will be able to cope with some of this frustration. The key factor is that reaching your new goals must bring you genuine satisfaction. If your new goals are not authentic, the frustration of not having reached your true goals will remain and perhaps intensify. Two different people, a salesman and a lawyer, provide good examples of how changing your goals can help you handle a career reversal.[7]

Jack worked as a sales representative for an expanding company. Although he was not convinced that he had managerial ability, he aspired to become a sales manager in his division. When the position was available, it was assigned to another sales representative in Jack's territory. Jack convinced himself that he was not ready for the increased responsibility. Seven years later, he again was passed over with the managerial position assigned to a younger salesman with less experience than Jack.

At this point, Jack realized that he was never going to be offered a manager's position. To decrease some of his frustrations, he found other, more attainable, goals such as becoming an active leader in the Boy Scouts and developing expertise in photography. Both of these new ventures gave him the increased satisfaction and ego boosting he felt that he lost by not being promoted to manager.

Back in high school, Larry was absolutely certain that his adult occupation would be law. Seven years later, upon graduation from law school, he attained a position with a prestigious law firm. Disconcerting to him, Larry found some elements of law practice to be distasteful. He felt particularly uncomfortable arguing with other lawyers and kowtowing to clients. (Of course, this is Larry's perception of law practice and not a perception shared by most lawyers.) The partners of the firm realized this about him and gladly accepted Larry's resignation when it was offered. They gave him the constructive advice that he should seek another area in which to utilize his remarkable intellectual capability.

Larry decided that working as a law professor might fit his preferences more than the practice of law. After completing some additional graduate work, Larry secured a teaching position with a large southern law school. He has since earned himself a reputation as an expert on laws related to ecology. At one point he was interviewed by former President, Jimmy Carter, for a position in the Department of Energy. At last report, Larry is quite content with his professional life.

"Change Goals" is a self-evident form of the defense mechanism, substitution. Since what you are doing now leads to frustration, you seek a constructive substitute goal.

LOOK FOR SIGNALS OF GOOD NEWS

A curious, almost mystical, way of bouncing back from job reversals is to receive subtle signals from the outside world. If you keep your mind finely tuned to the world around you, you will be able to notice these signals. Once they appear, you can face others with renewed confidence and realize that good news is imminent. Just as a bird chirping signals the end of a violent rainstorm, the world of work offers its own indicators of good times ahead. Not everybody gets the same signals, but here are a few that could mean the turning point for you:

- The Internal Revenue Service informs you that they recalculated your tax return. You and your tax advisor had erred in favor of the IRS. Therefore, a check for $288 is enclosed to you.
- You have been trying to see a key executive for over a week. One morning his secretary phones you and says, "Mr. Anderson will be able to see you at 11:00 this morning."
- A manager whom you insulted in a meeting last week smiles at you with forgiveness and invites you to join her for lunch.
- A prospective customer of a large account returns your phone call, asking to learn more about your product.
- You learn from the personnel department that you will not be cut in the next layoff.
- The new annual report includes a photo essay of employees at work. You are one of the employees pictured.
- Your request for additional clerical help is approved.
- Your rival for promotion resigns.

"Look for Signals of Good News" includes some elements of developing a positive mental attitude. However, it also illustrates the importance of staying mentally alert and sizing up your environment. Faced with the emotional turmoil created by personal problems, many people neglect to use their diagnostic faculties.

NOTES

1. Portions of this chapter are reproduced from or based on Andrew J. DuBrin, *Winning at Office Politics* (New York: Van Nostrand Reinhold, 1978), Chapter 12.

2. Case example researched by David J. Balonek.

3. Case example researched by Craig Carey.

4. Case example researched by Jim Smith.

5. Case example researched by Patricia Dillon.

6. William G. Ward, *The Student Journalist and Depth Reporting* (New York: Rosen Press, Inc., 1975).

7. Both case examples researched by Miriam Gould.

chapter ten
HOW TO HANDLE BEING FIRED

Why don't you have a seat? The reason I asked to see you this afternoon isn't a very pleasant one. Because of the recent downturn in business, top management has asked us to carefully review our headcount. Our payroll has just gotten out of line. Yours is one of the positions we're going to have to learn to live without. I'm sorry, but we have to terminate you as of December 31st. You can leave anytime you wish. You'll still get the full month's pay plus two months severance allowance. Do you think you could wrap things up by tomorrow afternoon?

This sombre message has been delivered so many times to so many different employees that it might profitably be sold on tape cassette. As the shock begins to sink in, the recipient of this message often asks silently, "But why me? Ninety-five percent of the other employees weren't asked to go. What was there about me that put me on the hit list?" Often the answer is that the fired employee did not meet the expectations of the position, was unable or unwilling to get along with co-workers, or was caught in a political squeeze play.

Whether you were let go for valid or invalid reasons, you are confronted with the task of managing a major trauma. For most people, being fired has an impact equivalent to divorce, serious illness, being mugged, or having your house burn down. Despite the gravity of the situation, many people do handle being fired admirably well. This chapter concentrates on the strategies people use to overcome the trauma of being fired. The emphasis is not on the mechanics of job-finding but on ways of mobilizing your energy and gaining control of your emotional turmoil.

TELEPHONE AN INTIMATE

If you've just been delivered the blow of "Sorry, you're fired," you need a quick method of defusing some of your pent-up feelings. The first impulse of many just-fired employees is to plea with the organization to reconsider. A typical request after being fired is, "Won't you give me one more chance? I'm sure I can do better next time." A typical argument after being laid-off is "Isn't it possible to transfer me to another department? I'm sure I can make a contribution somewhere else." Neither plea works. The organization has probably given considerable thought to giving you one more chance or placing you elsewhere.

Once the request is refused, the individual often develops a surge of anger. For sake of getting a good reference, it is best to find another outlet for your anger. Using co-workers for an emotional outlet is less than ideal. Since their hidden reaction might be "Better you than me," or "I think you deserved it," their response to you might be less than sympathetic.

A more rewarding course of action is to call your spouse, a parent, or a close friend. Although the phone conversation might be brief, this instant sharing of your trauma can be beneficial. After informing another person close to you that you have been dismissed from employment, the two of you will probably agree to discuss the topic at length upon arrival at home.

"Telephone an Intimate" is a constructive use of *catharsis*. You relieve the tension of being fired by discussing it with a person you trust.

TRY NOT TO PANIC

Once you return home, the real impact associated with being fired is apt to sink in. Now you are faced with the biggest challenge of dealing with involuntary separation from an employer. You must find ways not to panic. Asked, "What is the first step to getting back on the payroll after being dismissed?," a career counselor replied,

> The most important advice is negative. Don't panic. Realize that your job loss is a catastrophe from your own point of view, but that it will be quite unnoticed by the rest of the world. Share the news with your family and others you trust. Maybe you have children in college. Tell them: "You were joking about taking a job in the cafeteria. Well, let's not laugh about it anymore. It might be a good idea if you'd pitch in and help."[1]

"Try Not to Panic" is a straightforward, yet difficult to implement, suggestion about the importance of maintaining emotional control. Once your emotions are somewhat under control, you can begin drawing up a plan to bounce back.

INFORM YOUR CREDITORS

After you have shared the news of your temporary setback with a confidante, your creditors should be informed next (assuming you have not yet implemented the advice about getting out of debt given in Chapter 6). A counterproductive strategy used by many recently fired individuals is to ignore utility bills, mortgage or rent payments, car payments, and credit-card bills. A denial strategy like this can only backfire, leading to an intensification of your emotional turmoil. In addition to facing the problem of finding a job, you are forced to joust with your creditors.

A positive, sincere approach to creditors often results in a workable compromise that will help you manage some of the emotional discomfort associated with not being able to meet all of your current financial obligations. It is sometimes possible to make only interest payments until you get back on your feet financially. Sometimes an informal agreement can be made to extend the repayment schedule a few months. For instance, instead of having your car paid twenty-eight months from now, you agree to have all the payments made thirty-one months from now. Since you may have to pay those few extra months of interest, the lending agency does not suffer. Consequently, neither does your credit record.

Sometimes a touch of drama helps. You might say to a creditor,

"As this letter shows, I will no longer be on the payroll after next month. I know I owe you $600. I'll be paying you back the best I can as soon as I'm back on somebody's payroll. In the meantime, if you insist on immediate payment, I'll hold a garage sale and sell off anything I can to make my payments."

A credit counselor offered advice to laid-off United Auto Workers members, that has relevance for wage earners at all levels. According to him, "Chrysler Credit (or GMAC, or your bank) doesn't want your car. What if you're forced to miss a payment? The creditor cannot read your mind. They do not know what your problem is unless you communicate with them. They do not want to carry delinquent accounts. They want to work out solutions."[2]

"Inform Your Creditors" is an example of the reality-oriented behavior a person must pursue in order to effectively manage setback. It is a curteous thing to do. It also may help you resolve financial problems while you have no income.

RECOGNIZE THAT YOU ARE NOT ALONE

As with most traumas in life, there is some comfort in knowing that many other people have experienced similar misfortune. A curious fact about the world of employment is that as your level of responsibility increases, so do your chances for being fired. A good, solid clerk has more employment security than a capable, highly-perched manager. As one employment consultant puts it,

Don't lose heart. When you are fired, you are automatically initiated into a prestigious club—a club that includes on its rolls some of the most brilliant, successful people the world of commerce has ever known. I know the president of a billion-dollar firm who got the ax. Now he's president of a two-billion-dollar firm. I once worked for a multimillion-dollar corporation whose president proudly told me on the day we first met that he never would have joined his present company if he hadn't been booted from a position with this company's toughest competitor. That president considers his firing to be the luckiest break of his business career. Whatever you do, don't think your situation is unique."[3]

Since January 1, 1979, amendments to the Age Discrimination in Employment Act (ADEA) have prohibited age-mandated retirement below age 70 for workers in private as well as in state and local government employment. If you work for a firm with less than twenty employees, the Act does not apply. Despite this legislation, an increasing number of people are being gently shoved into early retirement at age fifty-five. In a sense, they are being fired in a polite way.

The way around the law is to pay people to quit at age fifty-five. Pensions are being set to make early retirement possible. One school system pays teachers a $6000 bonus to quit. Some businesses calculate that it is profitable to retire people early with hefty retirement bonuses because they are replaced with workers at half their salary.

In summary, if you add the new breed of gently-fired people in their mid-fifties to the people being fired for other reasons, the newly fired person has substantial company.

"Recognize That You Are Not Alone" is an indirect way of relying upon the group for support. You will probably feel better when you realize that what happened to you is not grossly atypical.

SET UP SHOP

Once fired, the truly resilient person immediately goes into the business of finding another job. Often the job search is one of the most challenging assignments of your career. It is important to recognize that finding a new job requires sincere commitment. You may not be formally employed, but you should put in a full work week trying to find work. Dozens of vital tasks need to be performed in order to start once again receiving a regular paycheck, or bringing in a few dollars to help with interim expenses.

It makes sense to establish a room in your apartment or house as your job-search headquarters. Often, when a high-ranking manager is fired, he or she is granted the privilege of using a small office or desk space as a base of job-finding operations. A façade of this nature helps the ego of some people. For others the humiliation of coming to the office with no company-related job to perform far outweighs its advantages.

Here is a checklist of many of the major and minor job-finding tasks that need doing:

☐ Identify you job objectives by making a clear statement of the type of job or jobs you are seeking. If you have several job objectives in mind, it increases your chances of finding a job. An individual might have these job objectives: (a) public relations consultant, (b) communication specialist in a company, (c) public relations specialist, (d) community relations specialist.

☐ Identify several important things you might be able to do for the firm that hires you, such as "I can reduce your cost of sales through an efficient prospecting method I have developed." Identifying your contribution multiplies your chances of being hired.

☐ Prepare an up-to-date, polished resume, and have it printed. Most job-finding guides will provide you adequate advice about resume preparation. A poor resume limits your chances of receiving a job interview, which is the true purpose of a resume.

☐ Write a cover letter to accompany your resume. It should be a clear, hard-hitting, one- or two-paragraph statement of who you are and why you think you should be considered for the job in question—emphasizing what you can do for them! An example of a key sentence in one cover letter by a woman applying to a computer firm was, "I'm convinced I can apply my knowledge of computer software to help some of your clients solve their knottiest data processing problems."

☐ Make up a list of potential employers that you plan to contact through letter or telephone. Use trade directories, chamber of commerce directories, the yellow pages of the telephone directory, or a list of newspaper advertisements by firms in your area. Do not exclude local, state, provincial, or federal government agencies.

☐ Try to make at least six job-seeking telephone calls every day. Make up a list of employment agencies you intend to visit in your city or other communities where you would like to work. Include a visit to your state or provincial employment agency.

☐ If you graduated from a college or business school within the last five years, pay a visit to its placement service. Many employers who are recruiting for new graduates might be interested in speaking to a graduate with several years of experience.

☐ Call at least one dozen employed friends and acquaintances explaining that you are looking for a new position. A substantial proportion of job leads are turned up in precisely this manner.

☐ Purchase a ream of stationary with your name printed on both the letter paper and envelopes. While you're shopping, pick up one or two hundred postage stamps. You may need them all before your job search is completed.

☐ Get your job-seeking wardrobe together. New purchases can be avoided, but sprucing up old garments is highly recommended to achieve the successful look.

☐ Line up several references. For best results, ask people in advance if you can use them for a *favorable* reference. Ask a good friend to call your former employer, pretending that he or she is a prospective employer. Find out what kind of things the firm that fired you is really saying about you. Be ready to deal with any derogatory reference comments in a nondefensive manner when you are being given serious consideration for a position. (We will discuss this topic again later in the chapter.)

☐ Get outside in the fresh air for some exercise everyday. A tanned or wind-burned look is preferable to a prison-pallor when job seeking.

☐ Develop a bare-boned and sensible budget for your period of unemployment. For many individuals, severance pay will carry them for two to three months. Borrowing money while unemployed is difficult to arrange and fraught with payback problems.

☐ Invest some time in selling all your unwanted and no longer useful household goods. An average household can raise several hundred dollars through this method.

☐ If you think it's worth your time, visit your unemployment office to obtain the insurance payments that are rightfully yours. Unemployment compensation *is* a form of insurance. You and your previous employers have been paying premiums on this for years.

"Set Up Shop" is a pure example of problem-solving behavior when faced with adversity. Here you make full use of the problem-solving method. Once you find a job you can evaluate the outcome of your decision.

TAKE JOB-FINDING BOOKS AND MANUALS SERIOUSLY

While unemployed many people will spend hundreds of dollars travelling to job interviews, and even more money on recreation to help relieve the tension of job-finding. Yet few people will invest three to ten dollars to purchase a well-documented, well-researched book about job finding. The business section of most book stores or libraries is stocked with job-finding guides. Such books amplify the fifteen suggestions previously discussed along with providing a substantial amount of additional information to help you become employed or find a better job.

A possible criticism of several job-finding books is that they advise against preparing a resume. Instead, you are supposed to demand an interview and sell yourself in person. The reality is that most employers demand to see a resume before they will grant you an interview. Personnel departments are particularly adamant about this procedure.

Purchasing a job-finding guide only can help you if you follow those suggestions which seem the most applicable to you. Sometimes, unemployed people are so despondent or unnerved that they cannot focus on written advice. If this is your situation, calm down before embarking on your job search. Speak to a friend, counselor, pastor, or family physician. Get back in control before blowing some good job leads. One man was in such emotional turmoil that he said to his first prospective employer, "You've got to hire me. If I don't start working this month, I'll lose both my house and my car." The manager conducting the interview advised the personnel department to send on another applicant. He reasoned, "The last guy was too desperate. He frightened me."

"Take Job-finding Books and Manuals Seriously" illustrates again the importance of staying intellectually alert despite the emotional turmoil facing you. Reading this material can be tension reducing.

ADMIT YOU WERE FIRED

A question on the minds of most people who have been fired is "Should I tell an interviewer that I was fired?" It is ordinarily believed that admitting you were fired automatically removes you from further consideration. Not admitting that you were fired is an immature decision. Reference checking by the prospective employer will usually reveal the fact that you were dismissed involuntarily. It is therefore wise to tell the truth.

Admitting you were fired, or asked to resign, does not exempt you from having to furnish a plausible explanation of what happened. A guiding principle is to take the initiative to explain the circumstances of your dismissal without being self-abasing or unduly critical of your past employer.

Assume that you have been asked to resign because your boss thought you moved too slowly on projects and that you took too long to make a decision. You might tell the interviewer something to the effect,

> My last boss and I had a very different approach to the job. He is a very intelligent man and a good manager, but also very quick on the trigger. With my background in accounting, I prefer to not commit myself to a course of action until the facts about a problem are solidly established. He was the opposite. He would prefer an off-the-cuff answer to my properly researching a problem. My previous boss, however, was quite content with my approach to making decisions. As you can see from my resume, I received two promotions in four years with that firm.
>
> It will be interesting to hear what my most recent boss tells you about me. I suspect his version of why he asked me to resign should coincide exactly with what I've told you. I'm really quite proud of my deliberate approach to making decisions.

"Admit You Were Fired" is a reminder to try to overcome the tendency toward denial and fantasy when under the pressure of unemployment. Most skilled interviewers spot defensive behavior quickly, and your defensiveness will arouse suspicion about your competence. This suspicion will hurt you in competing for potential jobs.

CAPITALIZE UPON THE HIDDEN OPPORTUNITY

An extraordinary fact about being fired is that it often represents a positive turning point in the careers of many people. Many an individual has expressed the sentiment, "If they didn't finally fire me, I would have stayed in that miserable job all my life. Now I'm free, finally doing what I want in life." Some people who basically enjoy, or at least tolerate, their jobs also benefit from being fired. Upon getting the ax, they move into a position which brings them a higher level of satisfaction.

The director of a career counseling firm that specializes in out-placement is convinced of the hidden value of being fired. He contends that when the initial shock of being fired passes, most managers conclude it was a blessing, an opportunity to step off the treadmill and ponder what they would really like to do for a living. A case in point is a forty-nine-year old economist who had worked twenty-nine years for one bank. The career counselor met with the banker immediately after he was fired. The counselor recalls, "The first thing he said to me was, 'What am I going to tell my wife?' Then before I could answer he said, 'Who is going to hire a man who's forty-nine years old and who's had one job in his life?'"

Like many other executives, this banker decided after he calmed down emotionally to go into an altogether different field, real estate. Today he is earning fifty percent more than he did during his last year at the bank.[4]

A modern trend is for people to have multiple careers during the course of their lifetime. It is no longer considered copping out for a person to enter a different career after having reached a reasonable degree of success in one field. Anyone tuned into the outside world has heard stories of the business executive who becomes a pig farmer at age forty-six, or the young corporate couple who give up their careers in a bureaucracy to open an antique shop, or the guidance counselor who leaves the school system at middle age to sell mutual funds.

Sometimes being fired serves as the impetus to start that long dreamed-about second, (or third) career. Peter is a case in point. He describes how he found his dream:

> It's all so simple in retrospect. I was a fifty-year-old senior executive in one of Canada's largest oil companies. My long hours of hard work brought me a churning stomach, a wife complaining that I was never home, and accusations of neglect from my children. I think the government benefitted the most. So much of my paycheck was eaten up in taxes that I hardly felt like a high-priced executive. To boot, handling the three mortgages on my suburban home made me feel like a pauper.
>
> Then one day I was fired unceremoniously after my oil company was merged with another. At first I started to look for a new corporate position, but then I decided it was time to cash in my chips and start a new life. With my family's blessings, I opened a boat hostel on a scenic lake in Ontario. I had accumulated enough money

during my corporate days to serve as a small grub stake. We also sold our house which gave us additional capital.

Business is great here. I make just enough money to feed myself and my family. We live in a well-appointed, year-round cottage. I've eliminated all the frills like life insurance and a second car. I work about seventy-five hours per week in season, with no complaints on my part. During the off-season, I mostly putter around. In place of the old business conferences, I hold pleasant chats with the boat owners who do business with me. Life is not without its problems, but I'm a lot better off than I used to be.

Capitalizing upon the hidden opportunity in being fired is not restricted to executives. Employees fired from jobs at all levels can sometimes break loose into a venture that is better suited to their preferences than life in a bureaucracy. One such individual was Bob, who had a high-paying job in a machine shop in an automotive plant in New Jersey. The plant closed down one summer because the company deemed it obsolete and unprofitable. The entire plant staff, from unskilled workers to top plant officials, were without jobs. In his late forties, Bob was concerned about finding new employment.

Discouraged after two weeks of job hunting, Bob held a mutual problem-solving session with three of his former co-workers. Encouraged by Bob's courageous thinking, the group decided to open its own machine shop. Part of their financial backing came from both the company and the union. All four workers were to receive ninety percent of their salary for twelve months. In addition, they were able to obtain a Small Business Administration loan. All in all, they had enough money to get started.

Bob, the most articulate of the four, concentrated his working hours on trying to sell the services of the shop to small firms who might be in need of their type of assistance. In a sense, they functioned as a work overflow capability for other companies. Bob's machine shop also contracted some business from small firms which lacked the kind of special machinery his firm had available. After six months of operation, it appeared that the four would be able to eke out a living from their business. As the oldest of the four commented, "Can't say I'll ever do as well as I did working for the company. But I do like the idea of finally being one of the bosses. It's a darn good way to finish out my working years."[5]

"Capitalize Upon the Hidden Opportunity" is based on a combination of using a positive mental attitude and finding creative alternatives. Going into business for yourself subsequent to being fired is indeed a creative alternative.

KEEP PRESSURE ON YOURSELF

One job-finding guide offers the sage advice of keeping pressure on yourself.[6] Before being fired, many people were in a job situation whereby they didn't have enough time to accomplish all the job and personal chores facing them. When you are between jobs, there is a natural tendency to back off from your usual hectic pace. Such a slowing down of your work habits could greatly delay finding a position. As described in an earlier section of this chapter, there are an enormous number of tasks to be accomplished when you set up shop to find a job. Here we are concerned with the inner psychology of keeping your foot on the accelerator.

An unemployed individual has to watch out for the lackadaisical attitude of enjoying the free time. Such an attitude can delay the job search. And remember that generally the longer you are unemployed, the more difficult it is to get reemployed. If your job search lasts two years, many prospective employers will regard you as a job-market drop out—somebody who is no longer mentally equipped to handle a job routine.

Aside from carrying out all the tasks mentioned earlier, and the suggestions found in at least two job-finding guides of your choice, there is one central task to be performed. Process every lead, however insignificant it might seem at the time. Any employment agency recommended to you is worth contacting; get in touch with any executive whose name is offered to you by a friend; answer all correspondence, however non-committal it might sound.

Ram, a food technologist, had been out of work for five months, during a slow period in the economy. Rejection after rejection piled up. The story was usually similar, "We are impressed with your background, but right now we are faced with a tight squeeze on employ-

ment." Discouraged, but not defeated, Ram poured over his meager list
of leads. An unusual letter from a medium-size food processor near
Honolulu, suggested that he drop in for a visit should he be in Hawaii.
(Ram was living in Montreal at the time.) He decided to invest a portion
of his dwindling funds in a trip to Honolulu and take the company up on
the "drop by when you're in town" offer.

Once in town, Ram phoned the company in question. The personnel officer Ram was referred to was quite surprised that he actually
acted upon this casual invitation, considering the cost of airfare between Montreal and Honolulu. The personnel officer listened to Ram's
story, then sheepishly admitted

> Your background certainly fits our needs, but the food industry is
> in kind of a budget crunch these days. We're only hiring a few
> production workers right now. We have nothing for a person at
> your level. However, since you have come all the way out here to
> visit us, let me introduce you to one of the people whom you would
> work for, should an opening develop.

Ram was then introduced to the chief process engineer who offered to
take him to lunch. Taking an immediate liking to Ram, the chief told
him over a drink,

> I feel guilty as hell for what the firm did. We invited you out here
> without volunteering to pay your expenses. I can't change com-
> pany policy, but I think I can make it up to you. Over the weekend,
> my counterpart in a smaller food processor told me his only food
> technologist decided to quit. It seems that the woman has decided
> to do something else with her career. I'll call him when we get back
> from lunch. Maybe you can be interviewed for that job before they
> post the vacancy or advertise it in a newspaper.

By 4:30 P.M. that day Ram had his interview at the other company.
Twenty-four hours later, Ram was headed back to Canada with a warm
feeling. The smaller firm told him they would be in touch within one
week, informing him of their decision. Within a few days, the operations
vice president of the small food processor called Ram with the good
news: "We want you as our chief food technologist, starting salary
$31,500 plus benefits. Besides that we're reimbursing you for half your

trip out here. Can you start in two weeks?" Ram accepted. At the latest report, he has bought some stock in the company that hired him, is engaged to a Hawaiian woman, and plans to never return to a northern climate.

Processing every lead worked for Ram, as it does for almost anybody seeking new employment.

"Keep Pressure on Yourself" illustrates the importance of goal setting on a daily basis. Many people need structure imposed by others. While unemployed, you may have to create your own structure in the form of daily and weekly goals.

SHARE YOUR BURDEN WITH YOUR FRIENDS

Bouncing back from being fired can be a lonely experience. Each day turns up its own joys and disappointments. A phone call to a friend to update him or her on your job search can be a useful way of dealing with your emotion. It's good to get somebody else (perhaps in addition to your spouse or partner) to share in the excitement of a good lead turned up and the despair of another dejection. A particularly invaluable friend is someone who has successfully handled being fired.

A curious form of loneliness when between jobs stems from the fact that many colleagues do not want you around. People with terminal illnesses often face the same plight. As one communications director puts it, "If there ever was a time to call a friend, this is it. Managers who have felt the loneliness of being fired are often puzzled by their colleague's silence."[7]

One manager who was recently fired observes that one of the worst things is that no one wants to associate with him anymore. He claims that friends and professional acquaintances became so uncomfortable around him that he ceased going out just to avoid the awkward confrontations.[8]

"Share your Burdens with Your Friends" is a straightforward combination of receiving emotional support and catharsis.

REMEMBER THAT YOU'RE ONLY LOOKING
FOR ONE JOB

Almost anybody forced to search for a new job will experience substantial amounts of rejection. You may be considered overqualified by some prospective employers and underqualified by others. Some places will tell you a job has just been filled when you know from an inside source that the job is still vacant. You must consider rejection to be part of the job-hunting game. Matching available people with available jobs is a cumbersome system. People are rejected for both logical and emotional reasons.

A manager who had been through the painstaking process of finding new employment was invited to speak to a group of unemployed managers and professionals. (The group is known as Forty Plus and has branches throughout the country.) The man spoke with verve about how 275 companies had either ignored his job-seeking letter or rejected him after a job interview. In disbelief, a member of the audience said angrily, "How can you be so happy when you swallowed all that rejection? Don't you have any pride?"

"True, I was rejected or ignored by 275 companies," responded the manager. "But the 276th made me an offer. And I was only looking for one job."

"Remember That You're Only Looking for One Job" might be interpreted as an example of the expectancy theory of motivation. You will keep trying if you believe that what you are doing is the right action to find a job. You may not get many positive responses, but you need only one.

NEXT TIME, PREPARE IN ADVANCE
AND WATCH FOR WARNING SIGNALS

Now that you've followed the advice in this chapter, you could be happily esconced in a new position. Despite your present state of euphoria, do not discard that job-finding file you have so carefully put together. Do not throw away the names of all those valuable contacts you have developed. Do not ignore that network of people who gave you some assistance. Continue to cultivate your sources from time to time. Offer help to others whom you know are themselves now out of work. You never know when you may be forced to look for another position again. Keep your job-searching skills honed.

An important part of preparing in advance is to stay alert to early warning signals that you are close to being fired. If these signals are present, get some verification. If it is true that your days on the job are numbered, look for another job before you are formally axed. Not every place of work has the same bad news signals, but here are some common ones that warn you when you're a prime candidate for the firing line:

- Your in-basket gets lighter and lighter although your job has not changed. It is beginning to appear that you are being given less and less to do.
- The flow of interoffice memos being sent to your attention dwindles.
- You are almost never invited to a meeting outside your department.
- Your boss never asks you your opinion on any situation of consequence.
- An internal or external consultant asks you to fill out a questionnaire defending the value of your job. The consultant informs you that this is merely part of a "study."
- Nobody of higher rank invites you to lunch any longer.
- You're moved into a smaller office, or an office without a window.
- You're asked to explain your job to a "trainee" when an on-the-job training program never existed in your department before.[9]

If many of these signals are present, and nobody will give you concrete assurance that your job is not in jeopardy, begin your job search immediately. In this way you might bounce back without having experienced the displeasure of being bounced out.

"New Time, Prepare in Advance and Watch for Warning Signals" illustrates both the importance of planning as a way of life and the value of maintaining a diagnostic viewpoint. If you look for particular signs, you may be able to head off adversity before it strikes.

NOTES

1. "If the Boss Says: 'You're Fired!'" *U.S. News & World Report*, March 12, 1979, p. 59.

2. "Laid-off Workers Get Tips On Coping," Associated Press story appearing in Rochester *Democrat and Chronicle*, July 20, 1980, p. 11 A.

3. Richard A. Payne, *How to Get A Better Job Quicker, New Expanded Edition* (New York: Taplinger Publishing Co., Inc., 1979), p. 155. ©1979 by Richard Payne. Reprinted by permission.

4. Jane See White, "Losing Job is Sometimes Blessing in Disguise," Associated Press story in Rochester *Democrat and Chronicle*, November 19, 1978, p. 23C.

5. Case example researched by Melissa Volk.

6. Payne, p. 156.

7. Elizabeth K. Kellar, "What Every Manager Should Know About Being Fired," *Public Management*, February 1979, p. 2.

8. *Ibid.*

9. Several items in this list are based on quotes from Robert Half in "Getting Fired: One View and Some Warning Signs," Rochester *Democrat and Chronicle*, September 18, 1977, p. 22C.

chapter eleven
OVERCOMING JOB BURNOUT

An adversity that you may face, if you are a conscientious worker, is job burnout. This widely discussed condition stems from working with people under stressful conditions, particularly when you are not receiving the rewards you think you deserve. Job burnout first was noticed in people who worked as social workers, case workers, police workers, ambulance medics, and school teachers. Recent evidence suggests that managers in business and government agencies also can become victims of job burnout. Anytime your job involves a good deal of conflict with others, and your rewards fall short of your expectations, you are a prime candidate for job burnout.

A spate of symptoms have been associated with job burnout. In general, a true case of job burnout seems like a mixture of depression and paranoia. You become listless, apathetic, exhausted, and angry. At the same time you are often quite suspicious of the motives of others. One military psychiatrist developed job burnout himself. Aside from daily grumbling about his discontent, he developed a standard greeting to new patients that was a tipoff to his burnout. Conditioned to think that each new patient was out to manipulate him, his opening line was "Okay, what do you want from me?" In his pre-burnout days, the same psychiatrist used a greeting something like, "How can I help you?"

Job burnout, unfortunately, also is associated with psychosomatic disorders. The burnout victim develops stress symptoms in addition to the negative attitudes already mentioned. One police worker resigned the force because he could no longer tolerate the stomach pains he experienced when dealing with homicides and child batterings.

As serious as burnout sounds, it can sometimes be dealt with successfully by tactics other than (or in addition to) consultation with a mental health professional. Most of the tactics to be described in this chapter focus on overcoming burnout that has already taken place. Some of these same tactics, as well as a few others to be mentioned, also are geared toward organizing your worklife so you can avoid job burnout.[1]

TAKE THE PROBLEM SERIOUSLY

Unfortunately, many career persons are reluctant to admit to themselves that they are experiencing burnout. They deceive themselves into believing that the situation will pass away, in the same way that many bodily aches and ailments disappear. Until you admit that your lethargy, apathy, and indifference is a problem calling for remedial action the process of recovery will be blocked. The strategy recommended is to be honest with yourself about the problem. Attending a burnout workshop, or visiting a psychotherapist or counselor can be a useful tactic.

The consequences of not taking burnout seriously could very well be a lifelong case of the occupational blahs. The burntout professional ultimately becomes extremely cynical.

"Take the Problem Seriously" is another application of the psychological concept of being open and honest with yourself. Instead of suppressing your feelings about burnout, you accept these feelings and begin the recovery process by confronting the problem.

PRACTICE RELAXATION TECHNIQUES

Burnout and stress are so closely related that it is difficult to figure out which one comes first. One viewpoint is that if you are burnt out, it brings about an internal stress reaction. The other viewpoint is that since you are under stress (such as dealing with ungrateful clients everyday), you experience burnout. Either way, it is important that you practice stress-reduction techniques to help you deal with the tensions that surround burnout. It is best to choose stress management techniques that are life enhancing such as physical exercise, meditation, or sexual relations. An ever-present danger is that the burnout victim will choose a method of stress reduction that actually contributes to the problem. A team of two psychologists, studying burnout among police workers, made these observations:

> For the cop, having a drink with his buddies after work may be a *decompression routine* offering a chance to unwind from the emotional pressures of the job, talk over worries and problems with trusted friends, and just laugh and have some fun. The important social function of drinking with the guys is often recognized by wives, although they sometimes long for alternative mechanisms that don't run the risk of alcoholism. "They need encounter groups besides the bar," as one wife put it. And, of course, when they are out with the guys, they are not with the family.[2]

"Practice Relaxation Techniques" is a well-researched strategy based upon current knowledge about stress management. Almost any competitive or serious-minded person would benefit from relaxation techniques. Relaxation will take your mind off your problem temporarily and make your life somewhat fuller.

SWITCH ASSIGNMENTS

A quick, and often very effective, method for bouncing back from burnout is to switch jobs or work assignments. If you are a social worker you may escape some of your problems by switching to an assignment that involves mostly administrative work and a minimum of direct contact with clients. If you are a plant manager, you may ask to be rotated to a straight engineering or sales position. Job rotation (the formal term for switching assignments) often brings about a new perspective, and it prevents the staleness which often contributes to burnout.

According to one authority on burnout, "Varying assignments and routines so that a worker can spend at least part of the time on work with a definite end or 'closure,' is helpful because long periods of working without visible results makes a fertile environment for burn-out."[3] Switching assignments is infrequently under your control, but at least you can bring up the topic to your boss.

"Switch Assignments" relates to the normal psychological need for variety and novelty as a way of avoiding apathy. Switching to assignments that provide closure also illustrates the utility of feedback for avoiding unpleasant mental states.

ALTER WORKING CONDITIONS

Sometimes a constructive way of alleviating burnout is to modify job conditions, thereby lessening the problem. Often this modification can be made for a group of workers. Again, this type of juggling may not be under your control, but perhaps you can bring the problem up in a staff meeting for management to consider. One hospice for dying patients was faced with an unacceptably high turnover rate among nurses. Management intervened by giving the nurses places away from patients to eat lunch and take breaks. Previously, they were forced into the uncomfortable arrangement of sharing lunches and cafeterias with the dying patients. In that hopeless environment, the nurses had limited opportunity to offer each other peer support or advice and encourage-ment. After this altered working condition, the turnover rate fell to a more acceptable level.[4]

"Alter Working Conditions" is often the result of clarifying the problem. With a little investigating, you may discover that the surface cause of burnout is poor working conditions.

DEVELOP REALISTIC EXPECTATIONS

A management training specialist, Ivan, was the quickest victim of burnout known to me. After two months in his position, he began to exhibit the classic symptoms of burnout—apathy, irritability, and disap-pointment. The sudden onset of his condition seemed closely tied in with his unrealistic expectations of what he could accomplish on his job. Ivan describes what happened in these terms:

> Was I deceived! My first assignment as management training specialist was to conduct a leadership training program for middle managers. I thought I would hit them with some of the latest developments in leadership theory and practice. My boss and higher management liked the basic idea of my program and gave me the green light. Once the programs actually began I knew something was wrong.

> Some of the managers yawned during the sessions. They laughed; they joked; they bragged about having stayed up half the night. A few of them patronized me. One woman in her fifties told me that after I had some practical knowledge under my belt, I would become a first rate trainer.

> I realized that only one out of ten trainees were really interested in the program. Since everybody assigned to the training program was a manager, I figured that they would automatically be interested in leadership theory. I thought they would be eager to sop up any information I could give them. I was crushed by their lack of response.

"Develop Realistic Expectations" is a variation of the well-documented strategy of *realistic goal-setting*. If your expectations are pitched at the right level, you might avoid some of the frustration that contributes to burnout.

REALIGN GOALS

Another strategy to overcome job burnout, which is related to developing realistic expectations, is to realign your goals once it appears they are too difficult to achieve. For instance, in the future, Ivan might strive to capture the interest of one-third of his trainees, not all of them. Hundreds of case workers have burnt out because they expected poor people to take their admonitions about food habits and money management seriously. You can only save or change a small proportion of people no matter what your occupation.

Realistic goals can sometimes prevent burnout. Take the situation of Jim, an occupational safety and health specialist. He has come to realize that despite the importance of safety and health on the job, not everybody is sold on the topic. He claims that he intends to fight one battle at a time, and will be happy if he has a positive impact on safety and health in his area. He puts it this way, "I can bang my head against the wall until the year 2000, but my company will never make safety and health its top priority. However, at least they are beginning to listen to me." With this attitude, Jim stands a good chance of preventing himself from becoming a victim of job burnout.

"Realign Goals" improves your chances of reaching them, thus bringing you an amount of satisfaction that could prevent a negative condition.

IMPROVE YOUR PERSONAL LIFE

An improvement in your personal life won't cure job burnout, but it could make the problem more bearable. In general, the best preventive measure against burnout is to lead a well-rounded life. Improving your personal life is a good starting point toward well-roundedness. Laird, a high school vice-principal, was experiencing traces of burnout. He had become irritated, annoyed, and frustrated with his position. In addition, he often felt exhausted at the end of the day. As vice-principal, he was concerned mainly with discipline problems and minor administrative chores considered too unimportant for the principal, yet too important for the principal's secretary. He applied, unsuccessfully, for a series of principal positions in other schools. Still his annoyance, and tinges of apathy toward his job persisted.

Divorced for six years, Laird was leading a dull social life. Quite suddenly, his social life brightened. A young woman was hired as a replacement for a social studies teacher who was ready to retire. She immediately took a liking to Laird. Although he was older than her father, she regarded Laird's chronological age as a sign of maturity and wisdom. Laird and Mona (the new teacher) developed a close and mutually satisfying relationship.

Laird's colleagues noticed that he now dressed better, looked more alert at staff meetings, discussed discipline problems with a more objective viewpoint, and looked upon minor administrative chores as challenging problems. As Laird said to the principal over morning coffee, "You're right. My spirits have picked up. Since Mona and I have been keeping company, little things don't bug me as much. Now when a teacher sends me a discipline problem that he or she should have handled, I look upon it as a learning experience both for that teacher and me. In the past, I would have acted annoyed and dragged my heels."

"Improve Your Personal Life" illustrates the concept that job satisfaction and life satisfaction are interrelated. Here the emphasis is on improving your personal life in order to improve your ability to cope with job frustrations.

TRY NEW ACTIVITIES

The more well-rounded your life is, the more protected you are against burnout, contends a psychoanalyst who specializes in treating the problem.[5] This advice is similar to taking a vacation when things are not going well for you. New activities would include hobbies, sports, serving in the community, and patronizing different restaurants. Trying out new activities can contribute to your recovery from burnout. However, the strategy of trying new activities is merely a supplement to other strategies.

Trying new activities seems to work best in overcoming relatively mild cases of job burnout such as that experienced by Marlene. She had worked as the head librarian in her high school for many years. Although she was well paid and well respected, apathy brought on from job burnout was beginning to take hold of Marlene. She began to think that most of her students and the faculty members really didn't care about what she was doing. Finding a new job seemed like a remote possibility for the indefinite future. Marlene noted, "At $24,500 per year, my current earnings are too high to accept a beginner's job in another field. The last time there was a head librarian opening at the local university, the library received 200 resumes."

Marlene searched for a hobby that was far removed from the

main thrust of her occupation. Her decision was to invest in the stock market. Naturally, she took out a few books about the market from her library. She carefully studied the business section of the newspaper every morning. After asking five different people for recommendations, Marlene settled on a stockbroker to advise her and execute her transactions.

As Marlene began to show a profit from her initial investment of $3500, her enthusiasm for the stock market intensified. As she became increasingly knowledgeable about securities, her life seemed to take on a new dimension that even carried over onto the job. Marlene explains how:

> My knowledge of the stock market now rivaled that of the school economics teacher. In collaboration with him, I established an investment section of the high school library. We offered students current books and periodicals about investing. We also collected a current file of annual reports on local and some national companies. My hobby now was infusing some new life into my work.

It also appeared that Marlene's efforts were earning her more recognition and appreciation from a number of students and faculty members. Such attention was what she needed to help her from developing a severe case of burnout.

"Try New Activities" is related indirectly to the concept of the *self-actualizing person*. People who invest intellectual, emotional, and physical energy into many many things receive the satisfaction of working toward fulfilling their potential. These multiple satisfactions help prevent you from becoming overly disappointed because one aspect of your life is not fulfilling at the time. Thus you more readily recover from burnout or prevent it from taking place.

IMPROVE YOUR PRESENT SITUATION

Job burnout sometimes comes about because one or two major problems influence your total outlook in an adverse way. If you can get to the root cause and modify that situation, the other parts of your problem may fall properly into place. Improving your present situation is much less risky than revamping your entire life style. If your solution doesn't work, at least you can develop a holding pattern until you develop a sensible alternative. The strategy of improving your present situation is closely akin to altering your working conditions. Willie, a youth counselor in a neighborhood center, found himself sinking into a condition of job burnout. In talking about the problem he noted,

> The thing that drives me crazy is that nobody has any respect for my time. I might be in my office talking to a troubled kid, and another worker from the agency comes barging right in. Or another kid with a problem will interrupt us. I feel that I'm being jerked around without my having any control over the matter.

Once Willie talked over the problem, the solution became obvious. Although the agency was shorthanded, an arrangement was made whereby Willie's visitors were screened during the afternoons, ordinarily the peak busy period for the agency. A clerk typist would sit at a desk outside Willie's office, performing her regular work while also serving as a receptionist. Visitors and agency personnel were both requested to have a seat or return later when Wille was free to see them. After two months of this new arrangement, Willie noticed that he felt much less burnt out than in the past.

"Improve Your Present Situation" is a strategy that forces you to clarify the problem and discover what is really contributing to your burnout. Bouncing back from burnout usually involves both cognitive and emotional discoveries.

STROKE YOURSELF

Burnout is a form of mental depression. As with mild depression, a workable antidote is to pamper yourself with small rewards for things that you do right. Influenced by transactional analysis, this strategy of positive reinforcement is known as *stroking.* Give yourself rewards for a job well done, such as a luxurious meal. (I personally opt for a submarine sandwich accompanied by Canadian ale.)

Suppose you perform well on a people-related task, such as conducting a meeting that achieves good results. The world may not pay you a compliment, but you can tell yourself that you did a good job and therefore deserve to be complimented. When you do something well, buy yourself a new piece of athletic equipment, suit, jacket, or dress. In short, stroke yourself rather than waiting for others to reward or stroke you.

Stroking will help you in the same way that receiving a compliment helps you cope with an ear infection or an aching back. Little by little, nice things happening to you help you deal with a nagging problem. As you presently feel better about things, you might be able to tackle a grand solution in the future. The pleasant sensations you are experiencing are also helping you place your bigger problem, such as deepening burnout in proper perspective.

And now for a disclaimer. Stroking yourself, as with realigning your goals, has a built-in problem that should be considered. It often suffers from a lack of authenticity. Realigning your goals is sometimes perceived by the individual as lowering personal standards or copping out. To many people, self-rewards do not seem nearly as potent as those conferred by other individuals. It therefore behooves you to only reward yourself for a job that is truly well done!

"Stroke Yourself" is an example of applying positive reinforcement to yourself. You set up both the rewards and the schedule for dispensing them. Many forms of habit control are based on this same principle. Self-stroking can be a useful low-key method of helping you overcome some types of adversity.

GET CLOSE TO SOMEBODY, INCLUDING YOURSELF

A prominent psychotherapist suggests that closeness is the enemy of burnout, and distance is its ally.[6] The remedy to burnout therefore is to get close to yourself or others. If you are close to another person, you can share your problems with that individual (similar to the technique of recovering from being fired). If you are in close touch with yourself, you might be in a position to better deal with your feelings. In other words, since you have a clear perspective on your problem, you can figure out a way to handle it.

Despite attempts at definition, closeness is a vague idea. In common use, it seems to mean much the same as "getting in touch with your feelings" or "tuning in to others." Supposedly you can achieve closeness to yourself by such means as going for a walk in the country or desert alone. You may get close to another individual by listening carefully to that person.

A worthy feature of the strategy of getting closer to others, including yourself is that even if it doesn't help you rebound from burnout, it has probably done some good anyway. Both you and the person you have drawn close to benefit from an emotionally intimate relationship. Similarly, getting close to yourself is a sound strategy for personal growth.

"Get Close to Somebody Including Yourself", at its root, is based on catharsis. You get in touch with yourself by expressing your emotions to somebody else or yourself. It may sound vague, but it works.

FIND A NEW CAREER OR NEW JOB

For many burnout victims, the only real solution is drastic, such as placing yourself in a new job or career situation. In support of this strategy, one woman who conducts burnout workshop contends that the best way to overcome burnout is to undergo a complete change.

Finding a second career requires long-range planning. The economy can absorb only so many small retail store owners or freelance operators. Sometimes a long-term avocation can be converted into an occupation, provided a high level of skill has been developed. One manager had been handcrafting furniture since age twenty. By age forty-three, he tired of spending so much time working directly with people. He converted savings plus a bank loan into an initial investment in his own custom furniture business. He worked longer hours in his new occupation at slightly lower net income, but his psychic income increased dramatically. He enjoyed shifting the balance of his activi-

ties from so much concern with people to more concern with his furniture.

Finding a new job can also be an antidote to burnout, providing
the new job does not contain the same contributors to the problem as
did the old one. A burnt out guidance counselor may experience temporary relief if he or she becomes a personnel specialist. But after
awhile the exguidance counselor may feel unappreciated and unre-
warded as a personnel worker.

One manager dealt with burnout problems by joining a firm that
placed more emphasis on the development of subordinates. He felt that
in his previous firm the efforts he invested in developing subordinates
were largely unappreciated and unnoticed by management. (His burnout stemmed from the fact that he was not getting the rewards he
anticipated.) The new firm rewarded such activity. Consequently he felt
rejuvenated in his new position.

"Find a New Career or New Job" makes full use of the problem-
solving method. It is based on the premise that environment or
situation has a profound influence on your behavior. Improve
your situation and you might overcome burnout.

MAINTAIN A GROWING EDGE

A philosophical strategy for preventing burnout is to maintain a lifelong
positive attitude toward self-development and self-improvement. By so
doing, the individual continues to receive new rewards. The logic behind this strategy is that if you avoid going stale, you decrease the
probability of burning out.

Over a period of time the manager of word processing techni-
cians begins to hear the same complaints from her subordinates; she
watches person after person leaving the word processing center for
transfer, promotion, or personal reasons; she hears the same old rush
requests week after week. Under these circumstances, many managers
would experience burnout. Using the growing edge strategy, the word
processing manager would continue to develop as a manager and as
an individual. One month she might learn a new technique of disciplin-

ing subordinates. She tries it, and the method works. The manager thus receives the reward of self-satisfaction for having used a personnel technique which proved effective. Each new increment of personal development yields a new reward. Fed by a long series of rewards, the word processing manager avoids burnout.

Maintaining a growing edge could prove to be your most important technique of improving your professional effectiveness and personal vitality, and coping with daily adversity.

"Maintain a Growing Edge" is based on the assumption that bouncing back often involves moving yourself down the road toward self-fulfillment—a higher order psychological need.

NOTES

1. Some of the information in this chapter follows closely the presentation in Chapter 18 of my book, *Contemporary Applied Management* (Plano, Texas: Business Publications, Inc., 1982).

2. Christina Maslach and Susan E. Jackson, "Burned-Out Cops and Their Families," *Psychology Today*, May 1979, p. 62.

3. Jerry E. Bishop, "The Personal and Business Costs of 'Job Burnout'," *Wall Street Journal*, November 11, 1980, p. 39.

4. *Ibid.*

5. Herbert J. Freudenberger, with Geraldine Richelson, *Burn Out: The High Cost of High Achievement* (Garden City, N.Y.: Anchor/Doubleday, 1980), p. 175.

6. *Ibid.*, pp. 123–142.

chapter twelve
REBUILDING YOUR SELF-CONFIDENCE

An annoying aspect of most forms of adversity and setback is that they chip away at your self-confidence. The energetic fifty-five-year old executive who suffers a stroke often emerges less self-confident than previously. A similar loss in self-confidence is experienced without warning by the twenty-four-year old woman who is dumped by her fiance. If you have been depressed or setback recently, you may need to rebuild your self-confidence.

The superficial aspects of self-confidence are well recognized by most people. Specifically, it is easy to identify a person who appears self-confident. Much less is known about the inner aspects of self-confidence. This chapter deals with valid strategies for restoring or rebuilding your self-confidence.

SEEK REASSURANCE

Only extraordinarily self-reliant people require no emotional support or reassurance from others when trying to get back up on their feet. Getting reassurance from others should be a first step before you begin to utilize more complicated strategies for rebuilding your self-confidence. It helps salve your wounds and reinforce the fact that you are not fighting the battle alone. Ordinarily the support comes from a spouse, partner, or family members. Others pay for their emotional support by ruminating over their setbacks with a therapist or lawyer. Where, or from whom, you get your emotional support is much less important than the fact that you get it somewhere. For most people, coping with hard times is too difficult to go it alone.

How does receiving emotional support help you rebuild your self-confidence? It works quite simply. If the message gets to you that other people believe in you, you develop a higher opinion of yourself—which is synonymous with increased self-confidence. Marty, a plant controller, received the ax after fifteen years of good service to his company. At the request of his wife, the two of them took a week vacation before he began his job search. Marty reported, "Without Beth, I could not have moved so confidently into the job market again. It took her most of the vacation, but she finally convinced me that the company was wrong, not me."

"Seek Reassurance" is tied in closely with the importance of improving your self-esteem in order to cope with adversity. As your self-esteem increases, so does your self-confidence.

OBTAIN A FEW EASY VICTORIES

Self-confidence builds up as a direct result of success. The more little victories you achieve in life, the more likely it is that your self-confidence will be high. Correspondingly, the more lack of success you encounter, the more likely it is that you will have low self-confidence. After you have been through the wringer, it is a good idea to pick up a few easy victories. Regardless of the size, any conquest will help you on the road back to recovery. Suppose your big proposal has been shot down by higher management. You are disappointed, shocked, and your self-confidence has dropped a dozen points. A good way to rebuild your self-confidence is to submit several low-key ideas that you know will be accepted.

Most fields of endeavor, on and off the job, have a room for an easy victory or two. The key idea is to regain your normal level of self-confidence by recording a success. To illustrate the possibilities, here are a few such easy-to-attain notches:

- You have tumbled one quarter-way down a steep mountain while skiing on a difficult hill. The way back is to take a couple of runs on easier slope. You are likely to regain your confidence.
- You are a free-lance magazine writer who has run up a string of five consecutive rejections. Get in touch with the book review editor of your local newspaper. Inquire if they might be interested in your reviewing a book of their choice. The result might be a needed boost in your self-confidence as a writer, even if the fee is only $40.
- Three consecutive people have spurned your invitation to get together with them socially. Write them off and invite the poorest child you know to dinner and the circus or a movie. The appreciation you will receive will help you get back up on your feet in a hurry.

"Obtain a Few Easy Victories" is based on a relatively new theory called the *success cycle*. Each little success builds up your self-confidence which leads to a bigger success, which leads to more self-confidence, and so on.

ENTER A LESS COMPETITIVE ENVIRONMENT

An extension of the easy victory strategy is to place yourself in a less competitive environment after you are convinced that your present environment has you in over your head. A less competitive environment might be just what you need to regain (or sometimes to establish) a satisfactory level of self-confidence. Ray, a college student discovered that this strategy paid enormous personal benefits.[1] With the help of his father's connections, Ray enrolled in an academically rigorous school. Ray had been a bright high school student in a friendly, smalltown central school. In comparison to most of the students at college, Ray felt inadequate. He performed barely well enough to avoid academic probation.

Ray leveled with himself and his father, "I'm in the wrong college. Half the guys and gals I meet here were valedictorians from good high schools. I'm a middleweight trying to mix it with heavyweights. I've got to do something that will make me feel like a whole human being again."

Ray's solution was to enroll in a much less competitive college nearby his home town. He made the right choice. Studying no more than he had at the better known college, Ray became an A-minus student at the local college. He gloried in the praise he received from his professors and his parents. The punchline is that Ray graduated from college as a self-confident young man with a positive attitude toward building a career.

"Enter a Less Competitive Environment" is a strategy based on the same concept as "Obtain a Few Easy Victories." It centers on the importance of setting realistic goals.

RETURN TO THE HARASSING SITUATION

This multi-purpose strategy is potent as a way of restoring your self-confidence after experiencing a setback. If you can compete successfully in a situation that previously harassed you, your self-confidence will receive a big boost. The risk, however, is that the same situation may harass you again. Many an aspiring bronco rider has shattered both his self-confidence and his bones by trying once too often to stay in the saddle on a bucking bronco.

Tammy, a programmer analyst, is today a self-confident professional facing a promising career. Despite her present-day attitudes and action, she had a slow beginning to her career. At one point, she almost gave up on computer programming as an occupation. Early in her career, Tammy worked her best when not under heavy job pressures. She could do a good job programming if not placed in a tight situation. On a particular Friday, at three o'clock in the morning, she was called out of bed to hurry down to the office and help out with a computer gone askew.

Bleary-eyed, Tammy arrived at the office to lend her expertise. The problem facing her was that somehow the computer wouldn't work properly. Paychecks were being printed with preposterous amounts like $.05 or $98,750 (both represented one week's pay for a clerk-typist). Tammy was given one hour to correct the mistake. By the end of the hour she had made no progress and was close to tears. Much to her embarrassment, Tammy's boss was called in next. He fixed the problem, and patiently explained to Tammy where she went wrong. Tammy confessed: "Your solution is something I should have thought of. I was too shook up to think rationally." With a note of encouragement, Tammy's boss said, "Okay, now that you know what you did wrong, we'll call on you to help us with our next off-hours snafu."

Three months later, Tammy was called in at five on a Sunday afternoon to debug a computer program that was making preposterous errors. This time many paychecks were being printed in triplicate and quadruplicate. Although tense and worried, Tammy admitted it to no one. She concentrated as best she could, remembering the tips her boss had given her during the last computer foul-up. Within thirty minutes, Tammy had diagnosed and solved the problem.

Tammy reports,

> My rising to the occasion in that second chance was a turning point in my career. Once the computer returned to normal functioning, I felt I was on my way to becoming a true professional. In a sense I had overcome my fear of not being able to perform under pressure. Unless you believe in your ability to fix a program when the stakes are high, you'll never make it in this field.

"Return to the Harassing Situation" is akin to *desensitization*, a way of reducing fears (as discussed earlier in "Get Back on the Horse that Threw You").

START ATTACKING SITUATIONS AGGRESSIVELY

One problem with being defeated is that you become too timid in your approach to that and similar situations. The player on a basketball team who blew a last-second shot that might have won the game sometimes suffers a temporary loss in self-confidence. That player may still be quivering inside during the next game, and play tentatively. Lacking is the aggressive, decisive approach that won the player a starting birth.

Similarly, on the job, and in personal life, a valid antidote to a loss in self-confidence is to start attacking situations aggressively again. If you were demoted, and are upset and disappointed over it, plunge into your lesser responsibilities with aggressiveness and flair. As your positive approach begins to pay dividends, your self-confidence will probably inch back up to its former level.

George, a pharmacist, is a good example of this principle in practice. George was dumped by his wife of ten years, a woman he loved quite deeply. Somehow she wanted to leave George and the two children to "find herself." George's wife, however, was hardly a runaway. She still visited the children regularly and was cordial to George. For months, George stumbled and stewed. He felt inadequate and shattered. With the encouragement of a young widower friend, George finally began to come out of his shell. He joined two singles clubs, and made careful note of unattached women among his customers. George began to take the initiative to start up a conversation with any female customer whom he thought might be unattached.

Before long, George had carved out a satisfactory social life for himself. As his success in meeting women increased, he became increasingly confident of his ability to meet additional women. George presently feels that he would prefer to avoid any heavy commitment with a woman until his children are older. But over a span of time, his positive approach to dating has increased his self-confidence. As his self-confidence increases, so does his ability to attract women. George wrote himself the right prescription.

"Start Attacking Situations Aggressively" fits in somewhat with the notion of the importance of assertive behavior in life. As you learn to say what you want and go after what you want, you are in position to bounce back.

ACHIEVE SOMETHING THAT STRETCHES YOUR CAPABILITY

Assume that one big setback, or a series of setbacks, has made you doubt your own capabilities. You are beginning to wonder if you are really the capable person you once thought you were. It will be difficult to convince yourself that you are a capable, self-confident person until you collect some objective evidence along these lines. One highly recommended approach to restoring your self-confidence is to achieve something that stretches your capability. This strategy should be used after obtaining a few easy victories, as previously described in this chapter.

Hank, a fifty-eight year old insurance sales representative, suffered a heart attack that required a coronary bypass to resolve. Normally outgoing, Hank became reserved and retiring after the operation. He felt embarrassed that he could not be the same old fireball of the past. One night, in a particularly deep funk, Hank read an article about a group of heart attack victims who became marathon runners. Hank thought to himself that he too could become a marathon runner.

Hank had already been ordered by his cardiologist to walk five miles per day. He decided that each day he would convert more and more of that walking into running. Within eleven months, Hank could run five miles. In his pre-heart attack days, Hank had never accomplished such a feat. Three months later, something happened to Hank that elevated his self-confidence to a level that seemed just right for him. As he explains,

> You might call it the Big Event in my life. Pepsi-Cola was sponsoring a ten kilometer marathon in our city. I guess they do the same thing all over the country. Since I had been running five miles, I figured I could add another mile to that total, which would be almost the same as ten kilometers. I practiced for thirty days, every day running a little less than one block further. Marathon Day was scrumptious. About 58 degrees Farenheit, no wind, and blue skies. I think I came in about fourth from last among all the finishers. What a fabulous accomplishment, I completed the race, and I wasn't last. I've felt great about myself ever since.

An intellectual accomplishment also can be used as a self-confidence builder. Susan had encountered the adversity of losing her bid to become a member of the state assembly. The election night returns were particularly disappointing to Susan because she had received so much financial support from her friends and family. It also was acknowledged that she was much more qualified for office than her opponent. Despite the comforting exhortations of her loved ones, Susan's self-confidence was shaken.

Her strategy for bouncing back was to forget politics for a while and strike out in a new direction that would be more under her control. She decided to become a world's expert on something. One day she hit upon the idea of studying the history of writing instruments such as fountain pens, quill pens, and pencils. After two years of part-time research (Susan works during the day as a bank officer), she is presently ready to begin writing her manuscript, "A Natural History of Writing Instruments." Says Susan, "I don't care if this ever becomes a book that produces royalties. What gives my ego a boost is that I'm now the world's leading authority on a topic that is interesting to me. And it took me a lot of hard work to get there."

"Achieve Something That Stretches Your Capability" is one more method of bouncing back that capitalizes upon the uplifting value of moving toward self-fulfillment. As you feel a little more self-fulfilled, you simultaneously become a little more self-confident.

INVENTORY YOUR PERSONAL ASSETS

A fundamental reason why many people suffer from a poor self-image and low self-confidence is that they don't appreciate their own good points and strengths. The next time adversity has dealt you a blow that makes your self-confidence quiver, take inventory of your assets as a person. For purposes of giving your self-confidence a boost, it is much better to concentrate on characteristics you possess as a person rather than tangible assets such as money in the bank. In preparing your list of assets, try not to be modest. You are looking for any confidence-booster you can find. Asking the help of a good friend or partner can be useful.

An exercise of this nature is carried out quite frequently in workshops designed to increase self-confidence. Here are two lists, one prepared by a man, the other by a woman, to give you an idea of the kinds of assets that might be included on such a list:

LILLIAN
Good listener; most people like me; good handwriting; good posture; inquisitive mind; good at solving problems; good sense of humor; patient with people who make mistakes; better than average appearance.
ANGELO
Good mechanical skills; works well under pressure; good dancer; friendly with strangers; strong as an ox; good cook; can laugh at my own mistakes; great looking guy; humble and modest.

The value of these lists is that they do add to your self-appreciation. Most people who lay out their good points on paper come away from the activity with at least a temporary boost in self-confidence. When you have encountered adversity, there is a tendency to blame yourself and dramatize your personal liabilities. People who lost out in competition (in sports or in business) often interpret it as a sign of weakness. An honest job of listing your assets will often help bring the scales back into balance.

"Inventory Your Personal Assets" is a direct way of providing positive feedback to yourself. When you find out that your assets aren't as bad as you thought, your self-confidence might receive a needed boost.

ASK OTHERS ABOUT YOUR GOOD POINTS

An important supplement to listing your own assets is to get the opinion of others on your good points. However, this tactic has to be used sparingly and with people who are personal-growth minded. You should be open and ask another person his or her opinion of you. Tell the person that you are taking an inventory of your assets for a human relations exercise (the one you are reading about right now!). Since that person knows of your work or your capabilities, you hope that he or she could spare a few minutes for this important exercise.

For many people, positive feedback from others does more for restoring self-confidence than does self-feedback. It relates back to the psychological fact that how you value yourself (self-esteem) depends to a large extent on what you think others think about you. Consequently, if other people—whose judgment you trust—think highly of you, your self-image will be positive.

John, an assistant professor of political science, had just suffered a setback. He had been turned down for promotion by his superiors, who thought he had not accomplished enough solid research to be promoted at this point in his career. Feeling down on himself, and with his self-confidence a little shaky, John came up with a good idea. He thought to himself, "Okay, so I've been turned down for promotion. I'm still a first rate teacher. I think I can prove it. I'll ask my students for their candid, and anonymous evaluation of me and the course I teach."

Within the next week, professor John dutifully handed out course evaluation sheets to his eighty-five students spread out over two courses and three sections. The comments came back along with the responses to standardized questions. John had guessed right. As in the past, the favorable comments outnumbered the unfavorable comments by a healthy margin. Among the best self-confidence builders were "Professor Martin has made me realize how practical political science really is" and "I'm going to recommend that my kid sister take this course. It's a good educational experience."

"Ask Others About Your Good Points" is another strategy of soliciting feedback. This feedback, if positive, will boost your self-confidence, since it comes from an unbiased source.

DRESS TO FEEL CONFIDENT

Suppose you have been down on your luck. Things have not been going well for you and you recognize that a tough climb is required to elevate yourself to normal functioning. Furthermore, you are willing to grasp at any tactic that might be an easy way to regain your self-esteem and self-confidence. Under these conditions, you might try dressing in a confident manner. No particular style of clothing is recommended for helping you rebuild your self-confidence. You have to try different outfits that you already own, or purchase (or rent) new clothing, until you find the combination that does the job.

For most people, their best outfit is a confidence builder. For some people, this outfit might be casual attire purchased from a discount clothing store. For other people, this outfit might be conservatively tailored and expensive suits bearing a label with snob appeal. To many an adolescent, a confidence-building outfit might be jeans and an inscribed tee shirt. For still others, any clean, recently purchased outfit in their wardrobe enhances their self-confidence.

The point of all this is that if your clothing makes you feel inwardly confident, you will be better able to project a confident image to the outside world. However mystical it seems, projecting outer confidence begins a process that makes you feel confident. As others respond to you positively because of the confidence that you project, you will in fact become more self-confident. It follows the same logic that raising your self-expectations becomes a self-fulfilling prophecy.

"Dress to Feel Confident" is an application of nonverbal communication. As described, dressing your best makes you feel better, and you in turn send out silent messages that you are feeling confident.

RAISE YOUR SELF-EXPECTATIONS

Perhaps the ultimate solution to rebuilding your self-confidence is to convince yourself that you expect to regain your composure after adversity strikes. Try to talk yourself into a state of playing the role of a person who has just shrugged off a temporary encounter with hard times. Develop a positive mental attitude, using the various strategies suggested in this book. The skeptic might reply, "If I had a positive mental attitude or I believed in myself, I wouldn't have the need to rebuild my self-confidence."

Fortunately, the skeptic is only partially right. If you assume a role long enough, you begin to take on characteristics of a person who occupies that role. An effective, relatively new coaching technique is to have the learner visualize an expert executing a particular shot or making a particular maneuver. Horse riders are urged to visualize themselves jumping flawlessly over a fence; tennis players are urged to visualize themselves hitting thunderous serves deep to the opponents backhand, and students of public speaking are told to visualize themselves making a captivating, confident presentation in front of an audience.

Expect yourself to rebuild your self-confidence after you have been thrown for a temporary loss. In the process, you will acquire the ultimate skill required for bouncing back and handling adversity in work and personal life. The skill is the belief in your own powers of resiliency. You will find it to be a lucrative investment of your time!

NOTES

1. Drew DuBrin researched this non-autobiographical case history.

INDEX

FREE!!
BOOKS BY MAIL
CATALOGUE

BOOKS BY MAIL will share with you our current bestselling books as well as hard to find specialty titles in areas that will match your interests. You will be updated on what's new in books at no cost to you. Just fill in the coupon below and discover the convenience of having books delivered to your home.

BOOKS BY MAIL

320 Steelcase Road E.,
Markham, Ontario L3R 2M1

Please send Books By Mail catalogue to:

Name_____
        (please print)

Address_____

City_____

Prov._____ Postal Code _____

(BBM1)